Middle East

A Directory of Resources

Compiled and edited by

Thomas P. Fenton

and

Mary J. Heffron

ORBIS BOOKS

Maryknoll, New York 10545

Resource Directories previously published

Third World Resource Directory
Asia and Pacific
Latin America and Caribbean
Women in the Third World
Food, Hunger, Agribusiness
Africa

We began work on this resource directory in 1987—the twentieth year of Israel's occupation of the West Bank and Gaza. We completed the manuscript in January 1988—a month in which an average of one Palestinian per day was killed in Gaza and many, many more savagely beaten by Israeli military forces.

We mourn the dead and join our voices with those of concerned people everywhere in praying for a just resolution of the legitimate grievances of the Palestinian people and a lasting peace for all in the region.

The Catholic Foreign Mission Society of America (Maryknoll) recruits and trains people for overseas missionary service. Through Orbis Books Maryknoll aims to foster the international dialogue that is essential to mission. The books published, however, reflect the opinions of their authors and are not meant to represent the official position of the society.

Graphics Credits: Americans for Middle East Understanding, 45 (M. Saleh Attia), 64 (Khaland Sabri); Human Rights Internet, 13; Middle East Research and Information Project, 16, 17, 66, 67 (Kamal Boulata), 92 (Jumana Husseini), 96, 115 (Eid Muhammad); New Jewish Agenda, 95; *Ripeh* magazine, 52. All from the DataCenter Graphics Collection (dcgc).

LIBARY OF CONGRESS
Library of Congress Cataloging-in-Publication Data

Middle East : a directory of resources / edited by Thomas Fenton and
  Mary Heffron.
    p.   cm.
  Includes indexes.
  ISBN 0-88344-533-6 (pbk.)
  1. Middle East — Politics and government — 1945- — Bibliography.
2. Middle East — Study and teaching — Audio-visual aids — Catalogs.
3. Middle East — Study and teaching — United States — Societies, etc. —
Directories. I. Fenton, Thomas P. II. Heffron, Mary J.
Z3014.P64M53 1988
[DS63.1]
016.956 — dc19   88-1603
                                                              CIP

Contents

Chapter 1: Organizations *1*

Annotated Entries 1
Organization name; address; telephone number; organization's self-description; keyword descriptions of the organization's political and religious affiliation, region and issue focus, activities, and resources; and title of periodical publications.
Supplementary List of Organizations 14
Information Sources 16

Chapter 2: Books *18*

Annotated Entries 19
Author(s) or editor(s); title; place of publication; publisher; date of publication; number of pages; price; keyword description of format; description of content.
Supplementary List of Books 45
Information Sources 52

Chapter 3: Periodicals *53*

Annotated Entries 53
Title; publisher; address; number of issues per year; format (newspaper, magazine, or newsletter); size (height in centimeters); number of pages; subscription costs; keyword description of format; description of content.
Supplementary List of Periodicals 64
Information Sources 67

Foreword

During a recent trip to the Gaza Strip, a young Palestinian said to me, "Why don't you Americans protest your own country's policies in this part of the world? My future depends on it." A few moments later he added, "Yours does as well." My Palestinian friend was right. Consider these items:

• Three wars are raging in the Middle East: the Arab-Israeli conflict, the civil war in Lebanon, and the war between Iran and Iraq.
• U.S. naval fleets escorting reflagged Kuwaiti oil convoys in the Persian Gulf are placed in the midst of hostile actions between Iraq and Iran — actions which have already resulted in an attack by Iraq on a U.S. naval vessel, as well as attacks by Iranian forces to which the United States has responded in kind.
• The Persian Gulf is filled with naval vessels — many of them nuclear equipped. Many analysts believe that unresolved conflicts in the Middle East might provide the tripwire for broader nuclear confrontation.
• The Middle East is the major recipient of U.S. military aid — Israel is number one and Egypt, number two.
• U.S. civilian and military personnel in the Middle East have been killed in numbers unseen since the end of U.S. military involvement in Vietnam.

Meanwhile, the Reagan administration thwarts peace proposals coming from the region and ignores European peace initiatives. The administration has even acted to cut off communication with the Palestinian Liberation Organization — one of the major parties to the Arab-Israeli-Palestinian conflict — by closing the PLO information office in Washington, D.C.

Also troubling is the fact that peace and social justice movements, who doggedly persist in challenging U.S. policy-inspired injustice and military intervention elsewhere in the Third World, virtually ignore events in the Middle East.

Silence in the United States allowed Hitler to invade Europe and wage a holocaust against the Jewish people. The silence was deafening as well when Cambodians were massacred by one of their own leaders. Now, the silence continues as thousands of lives are being lost in the Middle East.

The reasons for this silence are numerous and complex. But it is possible to break the silence surrounding U.S. Middle East policy. Our colleagues at Third World Resources have provided us with an invaluable tool for understanding the Middle East—a first step toward action.

Indeed, this Middle East volume in the series of Third World Resource directories will be useful to a wide range of individuals and organizations seeking to understand this complex region. Authors with diverse and wide ranging points of view—Noam Chomsky, Arthur Hertzberg, Edward Said, Ronald Young, David Shipler, Walter Laquer, Irene Gendzier, Jane Hunter, and others—are represented in this important compendium on the Middle East.

Librarians, peace groups, Third World organizations, women's groups, high school and university teachers, anti-intervention groups, and many others will find in this directory resources covering virtually all aspects of the Middle East.

Gail Pressberg
Executive Director, Foundation for Middle East Peace
Director, Middle East Programs, American Friends Service
    Committee, 1977–87

Preface

This directory of resources on the Middle East is one in a series of twelve volumes on Third World regions and issues that is being compiled by the Data Center's Third World Resources project.

OBJECTIVES

Our aim in compiling this and all the other resource guides in the twelve-volume series is to meet five objectives:

1. To strengthen the ties among organizations that oppose the injustices in foreign military and economic intervention in the Third World by helping to dismantle the institutional, issue-related, and regional barriers that now divide these groups.

Educators and activists who take a critical stance toward the impact of foreign intervention in Third World affairs are unnecessarily divided from one another and thus not as effective or as mutually supportive as they could be. They are divided institutionally, by issue orientation, and by region.

Institutional walls separate church workers from academics, community organizers from researchers, and social studies teachers from political activists. Third World Resources seeks to breach these institutional walls by publicizing the work of groups in all of these categories and by promoting their resources through a worldwide network of Third World–related progressive organizations.

Ironically, *issues* also drive wedges among activist organizations. Nuclear groups work on freeze issues, but fail to appreciate fully the urgency of the work of Central America–support organizations and vice versa. While this might make some sense tactically and while this focus of energies is perfectly understandable given the demands on the time of organizers, the lack of a network of mutually supportive progressive organizations clearly limits the impact of their work.

By putting people in touch with people—whatever the issue that may be their prime concern—Third World Resources encourages better cross-fertilization of ideas and plans. This results in more effective joint action and less duplication of effort in the production of education and action resources.

Regional barriers also fragment the resistance movement. Transnational corporations are — unfortunately — years ahead of their critics in realizing the need to have near-instantaneous communication across regional and national boundaries. Critics need to appreciate as well the importance of the broadest and quickest possible interchange of information and of plans for action.

Third World Resources transcends regional boundaries by including in this directory and in all its publications education- and action-oriented resources from all over the world. In this international aspect of our work we are helped by an international board of advisors and by our affiliation with Interdoc, an international network of research and documentation centers.

2. To legitimize and give equal time to alternative points of view on Third World affairs in general and on the involvement of the United States and other major powers in the Third World in particular.

In the United States critical analyses of the devastating impact of foreign public and private interests in the Third World are woefully underrepresented on library shelves across the country, and the challenging voice of oppressed Third World peoples is heard only as a whisper in the media and in classrooms. We suspect that this criticism applies equally well to other major industrialized powers.

— Yet analytical and educational work of this nature *is* being done. The array of resources presented in this directory testifies to that fact. This work *must* be publicized more widely.

— Critical Third World voices *are* crying out for justice. These voices *must* be magnified.

Commenting on the *Third World Resource Directory* the director of the Third World Studies Center in Manila has said: "The publication of the resource directory is truly heartwarming, for it tells us abundantly that in America not everyone has been silent or silenced and that many are laboring to explain the links between the behavior of the U.S. government and multinationals and the problems that we face in our own countries."

The purpose of the present directory is to publicize the efforts of those who are explaining these links and to make certain that the victims of interventionism by the United States and other powers have an opportunity to tell their story.

3. To promote the education/action resources of Third World–related organizations in a sustained, focused, and professional manner.

Data Center president Fred Goff described this problem in his Foreword to the *Third World Resource Directory:* "All too often the limited resources available to these [progressive] organizations are consumed by the process of producing a given book, pamphlet, newsletter, or film. Little energy or money remains for adequately publicizing these resources."

Anyone who has worked in solidarity and anti-intervention organizations knows how true this observation is. Even when the desire is there to reach beyond the institutional, issue-related, and regional barriers described above, the energy and financial resources that this outreach demands are too often just not there. This results in the under-utilization of available resources and — perhaps even worse — the waste of limited time and money in the production of redundant resources.

Third World Resources furthers the promotional outreach of progressive organizations by focusing its energies on *identifying* and *acquiring* resources from all over the world on regions such as the Middle East and on issues such as human rights, on *describing* and *evaluating* the resources in a careful, non-rhetorical fashion, on *presenting* them in an attractive, readily accessible format, and on *publicizing* the work of these organizations to a broad audience of educators, researchers, librarians, and political activists.

4. To put in the hands of researchers and organizers in the Third World comprehensive guides to Third World–related organizations and educational resources in other parts of the world.

Data Center president Fred Goff spoke to this problem as well: "Researchers and organizers in the Third World have learned from experience that information critical to their struggle for social justice — information about the realities of power in their own countries — is often available only here in the United States" (Foreword, *Third World Resource Directory*).

Third World Resources responds to this need of activists and educators in the Third World by providing them with handy sourcebooks of annotated descriptions and comprehensive lists of organizations, books, magazines, films, and other resources on a wide variety of Third World regions and related issues. The *Third World Resources* newsletter keeps these references current, and the Third World Resources documentation clearinghouse at the Data Center assures easy access to the entire collection of resources from anywhere in the world.

5. To direct concerned citizens in First World countries to the books, periodicals, audiovisuals, and other resources they need to study in order to take informed and effective action to correct injustices in the ways their governments and businesses treat Third World nations and peoples.

This directory and the others in the twelve-volume set are designed to offer immediate answers to the questions concerned citizens ask: How can I find out more about the impact of transnational corporations in Southeast Asia? What can I read to help me understand what is happening in the Middle East? What steps can I take to help people in the Philippines or to stop U.S. intervention in Central America? Where can I rent a good educational film on South Africa?

THIRD WORLD RESOURCES

The present directory and the entire twelve-volume set of resource directories update and expand the resources presented in the *Third World Resource Directory* (Orbis Books, 1984) and complement the two other facets of the Third World Resources project: a quarterly newsletter and resource guide and a clearinghouse of Third World–related resources.

Quarterly Newsletter and Resource Guide

Third World Resources publishes a twenty-page quarterly newsletter, *Third World Resources: A Quarterly Review of Resources from and about the Third World,* with notices and descriptive listings of organizations and newly released print, audiovisual, and other educational resources from and about the Third World. Each issue of the newsletter contains a unique four-page resource guide that provides comprehensive coverage of one particular region or issue. This resource guide is available at discounts for bulk distribution.

Clearinghouse of Third World–related Resources

In order to insure the widest possible access to the resources gathered in the course of work on the resource directories and newsletter Third World Resources catalogs and integrates all incoming information and materials into the library collection of the Data Center where they can be used by the hundreds of journalists, teachers, community organizers, and others who visit the center's public-access library each year. The materials are also available to the center's national and international network of Search Service clients.

In addition, bibliographical data on all of the resources are stored in a computerized data base to facilitate identification and retrieval of cross-referenced resources. Write to Third World Resources for information on how to gain access to this unique storehouse of critical information through the PeaceNet electronic communications network.

APPRECIATION

The work of Third World Resources is sustained by friends all over the world who give generously of their time, money, resources, and encouragement. This directory and all our efforts are dedicated to them with heartfelt thanks for their support.

We acknowledge in a special way the assistance of our colleagues at the Data Center and also the members of the Third World Resources Advisory Council. John Eagleson and the late Phil Scharper deserve the credit for launching this series of publications during their time at Orbis Books. Hank Schlau edited the manuscript of this directory with customary devotion to detail and Catherine Costello saw to it that the production train ran on time. To them and the rest of the staff at Orbis Books we extend our thanks.

Audrey Shabbas, Allan Solomonow, Peggy Thomas, Robert Staab, and Gary Lambrev were more than generous in sharing their time and collections of resources with us. We hope that this resource directory will further their efforts to build a just and lasting peace in the Middle East.

Grants in support of the production of *The Middle East: A Directory of Resources* were received from the Maryknoll Fathers and Brothers, the Middle East office of the National Council of Churches (U.S.A.), and the Middle East Liaison Office of the Presbyterian Church (U.S.A.). We are grateful for their generosity and personal support.

Introduction

The table of contents (above) is a guide to the overall structure of this directory. Each of the five chapters opens with an introduction that describes the format and contents of the particular chapter.

In this introduction we offer comments on the format and content of the directory as a whole.

FORMAT

This directory updates and expands the resources in the chapter on the Middle East in the *Third World Resource Directory* (Orbis Books, 1984). That chapter (pp. 122–41), as well as cross-referenced entries throughout the 1984 directory, should be consulted for complementary annotated lists of organizations and their resources on the Middle East.

We have tried to include complete descriptive and ordering information for every citation in this directory. Addresses for the organizations, publishers, and distributors appear either in the organizations index in the back of the book or with the actual entry when we have judged them to be necessary for the acquisition of resources. In some cases—such as in the periodicals chapter—we provide the address with the entry, for ease of ordering.

We caution you to inquire about current prices and terms of sale or rental before placing an order for any item in this directory.

CONTENT

Our comments on the content of this directory and of the resources themselves fall into three categories: definitions, scope, and political orientation.

Definitions

We use the term *Third World* in a geographical sense to encompass the peoples and countries of Africa, Asia and Pacific, Latin America and Caribbean, and the Middle East. In order to limit this directory to a modest size we have not focused on real and urgent concerns of persons who live in "Third World" conditions in the industrialized nations of North America, Europe, and other areas. We refer you to the sources of information in each of the chapters of this directory for indirect references to resources on those issues.

In contrast to our approach in the Middle East chapter in the *Third World Resource Directory* we have decided to include in this directory the five African nations that are north of the Sahara (Tunisia, Algeria, Libya, Egypt, and Morocco) because of their affinity with the nations in the area we traditionally call the Middle East.

Scope

In compiling this directory we endeavored to identify and acquire resources on the Middle East from organizations in all parts of the world. We acknowledge, however, that we still have a long way to go toward our goal of making the resources truly international in origin.

We realize that we have probably overlooked significant organizations and resources and that certain issues and regions have not been given the attention they deserve. We ask that you take into account the severe limits of time, funds, and geographical location within which we work and that you work with us to expand the reach of future editions of this directory.

Organizations were selected for inclusion in this directory because their work is predominantly focused on the Middle East. Concerns about the size of this directory forced us to omit organizations whose focus is much broader than that one issue. No directory on the Middle East would be complete without the education and action resources of organizations whose work is international or global in scope or whose focus of concern is only indirectly related to this one region. We urge you to consult the references given in the information sources section of each chapter for the names and addresses of complementary organizations such as these. See also the other issue directories in this twelve-volume set, all of which will contain resources on the Middle East.

We tried our best to identify and include resources on each of the countries in the region and on as wide a variety of topics as possible. It must be said, however, that the bulk of the resource materials available to us were concerned with the countries and issues that preoccupy the attention of activists, educators, journalists, policy-makers, and concerned citizens today. Those are the Arab-Israeli conflict and the human rights situation of the Palestinian people. Our selection of resources for this directory necessarily reflects these priorities.

Political Orientation

In the preface to the *Third World Resource Directory* we described the resources in that directory as — by and large — "partisan and biased" in favor of a "radical analysis" of Third World affairs. We described this radical analysis as one that contends that:

• reforms in the system are not enough; the crying need is for radical (that is, fundamental) changes in economic, political, and social (race, sex, and class) relations;

• change will come about through struggles (though not necessarily violent ones) between the "powerful" and the "powerless";

• the private and public institutional power of countries like the

United States is often used to frustrate initiatives for fundamental social change in Third World countries.

Even a cursory examination of educational resources about the Third World clearly demonstrates that most resources — and certainly the bulk of what we are exposed to in the media — ignore this "radical" analysis in favor of one that:

- stresses reforms that do not upset the present disposition of power;
- characterizes all people in the First World countries as rich and powerful and describes all in the Third World as poor and powerless;
- judges all struggles for radical social change to be Soviet-inspired and, therefore, to be opposed.

We situate our study of the Middle East in this "radical" political context. The resources we have selected for inclusion in this directory reflect the thinking of dedicated and thoughtful women and men who have come to the conclusion that genuine and equitable development in the Middle East demands *fundamental* changes in the status quo.

The sensitive nature of most political issues in the Middle East makes it especially difficult to hammer out an understanding of what these fundamental changes will demand of all the concerned parties. The resources cataloged in this directory all address the need for fundamental change, but they do not at all speak in unison.

While openly admitting our political orientation we feel it is also important to point out that political biases are woven into most — if not all — education and action resources on the regions and issues we are covering — whether those resources be left-wing, right-wing, or moderate in character. One cannot describe or analyze events in the Third World without betraying the lines of a political belief system regarding the means and pace of social change, the causes of social unrest, the allegiance owed one's own government, and so forth.

We have been straightforward about our own partisanship because we believe strongly that it is important for all to identify, evaluate, and admit to the biases that inform their analysis of and decisions regarding Third World affairs. Educators and librarians especially should be diligent about calling attention to the political biases in *all* of the resources on their desks and shelves — not just those that are alternative or radical in orientation.

In compiling a directory of alternative resources we are not advocating the wholesale substitution of one body of thought for another. For one thing, as a careful study of the resources in this directory will demonstrate, there is no "one body of thought" on the varied and numerous issues treated below — even though many of the resources could be labeled as alternative and politically radical. For another, a confession of one's political biases is not necessarily to be equated with a lack of appreciation for or openness to the truth in other points of view.

Our overriding aim is to promote the critical and responsible study of the alternative points of view represented in the resources in this directory along with consideration of all other descriptions and analyses of Third World affairs.

1

Organizations

This chapter is divided into three parts: annotated entries, supplementary list of organizations, and sources of additional information.

Each **annotated entry** includes: the organization's name, address, and telephone number; organization's self-description (in quotation marks); keyword descriptions of the organization's political and religious affiliation; focus (first geographical, then according to issues); activities; resources; and title(s) of periodical(s).

The keywords were selected by the organizations themselves and are intended to provide a quick overview of each organization's work. The descriptors are neither all-inclusive nor scientific.

If the name of a periodical stands alone, this means that complete ordering information for the magazine, newsletter, or newspaper is in the annotated entries section of the periodicals chapter below. Otherwise, pertinent descriptive information accompanies the citation.

Organizations in the **supplementary list** (pp. 14-16) are grouped under their home area or country: Middle East; Canada; Europe; and United States. Entries in the supplementary list include the organization's name, address, and telephone number, when all of this information is available.

Note that the two appendixes supply additional organizational information.

The part entitled **information sources** (pp. 16-17) provides the titles of directories and guides that contain the names of other organizations related to the Middle East.

All of the organizations and periodicals in this chapter are listed in the appropriate indexes at the back of this directory.

ANNOTATED ENTRIES

America-Israel Council for Israeli-Palestinian Peace, 4816 Cornell Ave., Downers Grove, IL 60515. Tel: (312) 969-7584. Washington represen-

tative: **Corinne Whitlatch, 221 Constitution Ave., N.E., Suite 21, Washington, D.C. 20002. Tel: (202) 546-8425.**

"AICIPP is a broadly based, heterogeneous group of Americans who share a common vision of peace in the Middle East based on mutual recognition between Israelis and Palestinians. We are from many walks of life—academia, business, the media—and we include many religious/cultural segments of American society: Jews, Christians, and others. We are proud of Palestinian participation in our leadership and in our broader membership.

"AICIPP was founded in 1982 to endorse the work of the Israeli Council for Israeli-Palestinian Peace, which was established in 1975. AICIPP believes that the best long range interests of the United States will be served by comprehensive Middle East peace and an end to the long-festering conflict between Israel and the Arab peoples. The heart of this conflict is that between Israel and the Palestinians, and this must be addressed directly. AICIPP supports mutual recognition by the Israelis and the Palestinians of each other's right to national self-determination."

FOCUS: Middle East. Human rights • militarism, peace, disarmament.

ACTIVITIES: Popular education • research and writing • networking • constituency education • distribution of print matter.

RESOURCES: Speakers.

PERIODICAL: *Voices for Peace.* 4 issues/year. Newsletter. AICIPP also distributes *The Other Israel,* the newsletter of the Israeli Council.

American Coalition for Middle East Dialogue, Stony Point Center, Stony Point, NY 10980. Tel: (914) 786-3887.

"ACMED is a coalition of dialogue groups throughout the United States made up of Jewish and Arab (Christian and Muslim) members, including Palestinians (and others). ACMED articulates its purpose as getting ready for peace, justice, and security in the Middle East. Individuals and groups who share this aim are welcome to inquire about membership in the coalition."

FOCUS: Middle East. Human rights • militarism, peace, disarmament.

ACTIVITIES: Popular education • networking • workshops and seminars.

RESOURCES: Speakers.

PERIODICAL: *The Dialogue.* 4 issues/year. Membership newsletter.

American Friends Service Committee, Middle East Program, 1501 Cherry St., Philadelphia, PA 19102. Tel: (215) 241-7000. See the organizations index for a list of AFSC area offices with Middle East programs.

"The American Friends Service Committee is a Quaker organization supported by individuals who care about peace, social justice, and humanitarian service. Its work is based on a profound Quaker belief in the dignity and worth of every person, and a faith in the power of love and nonviolence to bring about change."

POLITICAL AFFILIATION: Pacifist.

RELIGIOUS AFFILIATION: Society of Friends (Quakers).

FOCUS: Third World general • Middle East. Human rights • militarism, peace, disarmament • nuclear arms • women • international awareness • national liberation struggles • transnational corporations • social justice • native peoples • food, hunger, agribusiness • youth and militarism.

ACTIVITIES: Popular education • political action • research and writing • solidarity work • training of interns • media relations • networking • dissemination of documentation and information • production of audiovisuals • constituency education • policy-oriented research and writing • distribution of print matter • distribution of audiovisuals • workshops and seminars.

RESOURCES: Speakers • audiovisuals • study-action guides • research services • curriculum guides • books and literature • consultant services • library.

American Jewish Alternatives to Zionism (AJAZ), 501 Fifth Ave., Suite 2015, New York, NY 10017. Tel: (212) 557–5410.

"The educational program of AJAZ applies Judaism's values of justice and common humanity to the Arab/Zionist/Israeli conflict in the Middle East. In the United States we advocate a one-to-one human relationship between Jews and all Americans. In both areas of our concerns we reject Zionism/Israel's 'Jewish people' nationality attachment of all Jews to the State of Israel. These political-nationality claims distort constructive humanitarian programs. They are inconsistent with American Constitutional concepts of individual citizenship and separation of church and state. They are also a principal obstacle to Middle East peace.

"Our program, we believe, helps advance peace in the Middle East. It also prevents Zionist/Israel from successfully achieving its legislated objective of reversing the integration of American Jews 'by capturing the Jewish community' for its self-segregating 'Jewish people' nationality attachment of Jews to the State of Israel."

FOCUS: Middle East. Human rights • the Arab/Zionist/Israeli conflict in the Middle East • peace • full self-determination for the Palestinian people • establishment of a genuine democracy in Israel.

ACTIVITIES: Program of lectures • distribution of literature • cooperation with other organizations • popular education.

American-Arab Anti-Discrimination Committee, 1731 Connecticut Ave., NW, Washington, DC 20009. Tel: (202) 797–7662.

"The American-Arab Anti-Discrimination Committee (ADC) was founded in 1980 to defend the rights of people of Arab descent and to promote their rich ethnic heritage. ADC serves a national membership of Arab-Americans, joined by Americans of all ethnic origins, who are committed to challenging defamation, discrimination, and disenfranchisement wherever they occur.

"Through ADC, Arab-Americans make their voices heard. We protest defamation of Arabs and Arab-Americans in the media and in school curricula. We address foreign policy issues and legislation that affect our own well-being and that of our friends and relatives in the Middle East. And we promote and preserve the rich cultural traditions of our Arab heritage."

FOCUS: Middle East. Human rights • militarism, peace, disarmament • international awareness • national liberation struggles • native peoples • anti-Arab racism • Arab heritage.

ACTIVITIES: Political action • provision of legal services • grassroots advocacy • research and writing • training of interns • media relations • networking • constituency education • Congressional testimony • distribution of print matter • production of audiovisuals • distribution of audiovisuals • overseas project support • media monitoring • consumer protests.

RESOURCES: Speakers • audiovisuals • books and literature • action alerts • occasional papers • special reports.

PERIODICAL: *ADC Times.* 10 issues/year. Membership newsletter.

American-Israeli Civil Liberties Coalition, 15 E. 26 St., New York, NY 10010. Tel: (212) 696–9603.

"The American-Israeli Civil Liberties Coalition and our Israeli counterpart, Kol Koreh ('The Summoning Voice'), share the vision of Israel expressed so eloquently in this section of the Israeli Declaration of Independence: 'Israel will . . . foster the development of the country for the benefit of all citizens; it will be based on freedom, justice and peace as envisaged by the prophets of Israel; it will ensure complete equality of social and political rights to all its citizens irrespective of religion, race or sex; it will guarantee freedom of religion, conscience, education and culture.'

"The coalition came into existence in 1981 with three major purposes: (1) Keeping Americans informed about developments in Israel; (2) Promoting an American-Israeli dialogue on the crucial issues of justice and peace; and (3) Aiding Kol Koreh's programs with moral support, financial assistance, and the experience of Americans working on civil liberties education."

FOCUS: Israel. Civil liberties • human rights.

ACTIVITIES: Popular education • research and writing • media relations • dissemination of documentation and information • lecture tours by Israeli civil libertarians • workshops and seminars • overseas project support.

RESOURCES: Speakers.

PERIODICAL: *AICLC Newsletter.* 4 issues/year.

Americans for Middle East Understanding, 475 Riverside Dr., Rm. 771, New York, NY 10115. Tel: (212) 870–2053.

"AMEU was founded in 1967 by Americans from various professional fields (e.g., the first Commissioner General of UNRWA, the present Curator of Egyptology at the N.Y. Metropolitan Museum of Art, and the president of the Vatican's Pontifical Mission for Palestine) to help correct the negative stereotypes [of people in the Middle East] held by Americans and to present balanced information on the Israeli-Palestinian question. *The Link* has a circulation of 50,000."

FOCUS: Middle East. Culture, history, and current events in the Middle East • Arab-Israeli conflict.

ACTIVITIES: Popular education • research and writing • media relations • library services • dissemination of documentation and information • publishing • distribution of print matter • distribution of audiovisuals.

RESOURCES: Catalog • book club • Public Affairs pamphlet series.

PERIODICAL: *The Link.*

Americans for Progressive Israel, 150 Fifth Ave., Rm. 911, New York, NY 10011. Tel: (212) 255-8760.

"API was organized in 1948 to mobilize moral and material support for pioneering and progressive elements in the State of Israel. API identifies itself with the aspirations of the close to one hundred kibbutzim of the Kibbutz Artzi Federation. As Socialist Zionists we call for a positive and creative Jewish social, cultural, and political life in America with radical changes in community priorities and we advocate and support Israelis who propose mutual recognition between the government of Israel and any representative of the Palestinian people which recognizes Israel's right to exist within secure and recognized borders as called for in UN resolution 242 and renounces terrorism as a means of realizing political goals."

POLITICAL AFFILIATION: Socialist-Zionist.

RELIGIOUS AFFILIATION: Jewish.

FOCUS: Middle East • world Jewish affairs. Human rights • foreign aid and trade • labor • women • political economy • international awareness • national liberation struggles • social justice • Jewish-Arab relations • cooperatives and communes.

ACTIVITIES: Popular education • political action • research and writing • solidarity work • training of interns • media relations • constituency education • dissemination of documentation and information • workshops and seminars • overseas project support.

RESOURCES: Study-action guides • research services • consultant services • library.

PERIODICAL: *Israel Horizons. API Newsletter.* 3 or 4 issues/year. Membership newsletter.

Arab World Consultants, 2137 Rose St., Berkeley, CA 94709. Tel: (415) 845-6625.

"Arab World Consultants is the partnership of Audrey Shabbas, Carol El-Shaieb, and Ahlam Abu-Zayyad, whose combined backgrounds include *degrees* in anthropology, art, education, law (and Islamic Law), political science, social science, Near Eastern languages, and *experience* teaching, consulting, writing, editing, illustrating, as well as with living, traveling, and working in the Arab World itself.

"AWC has acted as 'culture broker' interpreting differences in language or communication style, value preferences, and lifestyle — acting as cultural negotiators for educators and institutions serving Arab immigrant populations.

"AWC's extensive repertoire includes the review of more than fifty social studies textbooks in current use, and the creation of a data bank of all types of media resources on the Middle East."

FOCUS: Middle East. Human rights • militarism, peace, disarmament • labor • women • international awareness • social justice • development • culture • values.

ACTIVITIES: Curriculum development • research and writing • dissemination of documentation and information • publishing • workshops and seminars.

RESOURCES: Speakers • audiovisuals • curriculum guides • books and literature • consultant services.

Association of Arab-American University Graduates, 556 Trapelo Rd., Belmont, MA 02178. Tel: (617) 484-5483.

"The A.A.U.G. is a non-profit, tax-exempt educational and cultural organization dedicated to fostering better understanding between the Arab and American peoples and promoting informative discussion of critical issues concerning the Arab world and the United States."

FOCUS: Middle East. Human rights • militarism, peace, disarmament • nuclear arms and energy • foreign aid and trade • political economy • international awareness • national liberation struggles • social justice • native peoples.

ACTIVITIES: Popular education • research and writing • solidarity work • media relations • networking • constituency education • publishing • distribution of print matter • distribution of audiovisuals • workshops and seminars • foreign service • sponsoring delegations to the Middle East.

RESOURCES: Speakers • audiovisuals • books and literature.

PERIODICAL: *Arab Studies Quarterly. Mideast Monitor. A.A.U.G. Newsletter.* 4 issues/year.

Churches for Middle East Peace, 110 Maryland Ave., NE, Suite 108, Washington, DC 20002. Tel: (202) 546-8425.

"Churches for Middle East Peace (C-MEP) was founded in 1985 to communicate to Congress and the executive branch [of the U.S. government] the perspectives and concerns reflected in the policy statements and Middle East exposure of participating religious denominations and church agencies [14 as of mid-1987]. We are committed to an even-handed approach that seeks security and justice for all peoples and countries in the region."

FOCUS: Middle East. Human rights • terrorism • the peace process • arms transfers • the unique status of Jerusalem.

ACTIVITIES: Legislative action • Congressional testimony • constituency education.

RESOURCES: Consultant services.

Al Haq (Law in the Service of Man), P.O. Box 1413, Ramallah, West Bank, Via Israel. Tel: (02) 95 2421.

"Al-Haq is the West Bank affiliate of the International Commission of Jurists, which is based in Geneva, Switzerland. Founded in 1980 under the name Law in the Service of Man, the organization adopted the name al-Haq (Arabic for justice, law, right, and fairness) in 1986. Al-Haq is concerned with the legal protection of individual and collective human rights and with developing and promoting the rule of law in the West Bank area. Its other objectives include providing services to the legal profession and extending legal aid and information to the non-legal community."

FOCUS: Middle East. Human rights • militarism, peace, disarmament • labor • social justice.

ACTIVITIES: Legal actions and aid • political action • research and writing • networking • library services • dissemination of documentation and information • publishing • workshops and seminars • human rights field investigations.

RESOURCES: Reports • booklets • handbooks • books and literature • consultant services • library.

PERIODICAL: *Al Haq Newsletter.*

Institute for Women's Studies in the Arab World, Beirut University College, P.O. Box 13/5053, Beirut, Lebanon. Tel: 811968.

"With a grant from the Ford Foundation, Beirut University College, long a leader in women's education in the Middle East, established the Institute for Women's Studies in the Arab World in October 1973. The institute encourages and evaluates research into the history, condition, and evolving needs of women in the Arab world. Based on this research, the institute engages in action programs to educate and assist the contemporary Arab woman, and in communications programs to transmit, regionally and internationally, a better understanding of the Arab woman — her traditional role, her place in today's society, and her aspirations and potential for the future."

FOCUS: Arab world. Women • labor • education • child development • legal and social status of women • rural development • contemporary Arab literature • career development.

ACTIVITIES: Research and writing • training of interns • library services • dissemination of documentation and information • publishing • workshops and seminars • teacher training.

RESOURCES: Library • research services • consultant services • books and monographs • research papers (unpublished).

PERIODICAL: *Al Raida.* 4 issues/year. Newsletter.

International Center for Peace in the Middle East, 107 Hahashmonaim St., Tel Aviv 67011, Israel. Tel: (03) 267399.

"Established in 1983, ICPME is an independent organization backed by a number of prominent national and international public figures and academics. It seeks to develop recommendations and promote educational activities with a view to the achievement of a comprehensive peace in the Middle East and it strives to help foster the equality of social, cultural, and political rights – individual and collective – for religious and national minorities in Israel."

FOCUS: Middle East. Peace in the Middle East • human rights • social justice • native peoples • equality of social, cultural, and political rights.

ACTIVITIES: Outreach to Israeli academic community • popular education • networking • policy-oriented research and writing • dissemination of documentation and information • publishing • teacher training • project support.

RESOURCES: Consultant services • discussion papers • English-language translations of articles from the Arab and Jewish press.

PERIODICAL: *Israel Press Briefs*. 12 issues/year. Press clippings.

International Committee for Palestinian Human Rights, 20 rue Dupont des Loges, F-75007 Paris, France. Tel: (1) 555 0149.

"Established in 1975, the International Committee for Palestinian Human Rights is an international organization of academics, lawyers, church groups, and others who desire to draw attention to individual cases of human rights violations affecting Palestinians."

FOCUS: Palestine • Occupied Territories. Human rights • unlawful deportations and extraditions • destruction of Palestinian property • closing of Palestinian educational institutions • forced resettlement of Bedouin tribes.

ACTIVITIES: Popular education • media relations • networking • dissemination of documentation and information.

RESOURCES: Reports and papers • consultant services • library.

International Jewish Peace Union, P.O. Box 5672, Berkeley, CA 94705. Tel: (415) 527–5003.

"The IJPU supports: (1) A just peace in the Middle East based on the right to self-determination of Palestinians and Israelis; (2) Negotiations conducted through an international conference, involving all parties to the conflict (Israel, the PLO, Arab states bordering Israel, the Soviet Union, and the United States); and (3) The two-state solution: the establishment of a Palestinian state on the West Bank and Gaza, alongside the state of Israel."

FOCUS: Middle East. Political repression • militarism, peace, disarmament • social justice.

ACTIVITIES: Workshops and seminars • popular education • dissemination of documentation and information.

RESOURCES: Speakers • literature.

International Organization for the Elimination of all Forms of Racial Discrimination (EAFORD), 2025 Eye St., NW, Suite 1020, Washington, DC 20006. Tel: (202) 223–2324. International secretariat: 41 rue de Zürich, 1201 Geneva, Switzerland.

"Established in 1976, EAFORD is an independent, non-governmental, international organization dedicated to upholding and promoting the International Convention on the Elimination of All Forms of Racial Discrimination, which was adopted by the General Assembly of the United

Nations in 1963 and ratified into law in January 1965. EAFORD has taken as its mandate to conduct, support, and publish scholarly research on racism and conflict. In particular, EAFORD investigates racism as it relates to the Palestine conflict, southern Africa, and the conditions of indigenous peoples in general."

FOCUS: International • Middle East • Africa • Latin America • Asia. Human rights • international awareness • national liberation struggles • social justice • native peoples.

ACTIVITIES: Popular education • research and writing • training of interns • networking • library services • dissemination of documentation and information • publishing • distribution of print matter • workshops and seminars.

RESOURCES: Speakers • research services • books and literature • consultant services • library.

PERIODICAL: *Without Prejudice.* 2 issues/year. Newsletter. $10/year (individual), $15/year (institutional).

Jewish Peace Fellowship, P.O. Box 271, Nyack, NY 10960. Tel: (914) 358-4601.

"Members of the JPF are a diverse group of people, religious and secular Jews from all our traditions and all branches of Judaism. All believe deeply that Jewish ideals and experience provide inspiration for a nonviolent way of life.

"We have worked to help end the Vietnam War, for the freedom of Jews in the Soviet Union, in Syria, Argentina, and Iraq, for the rights of Falashas and conscientious objectors in Israel, for a political solution and peaceful reconciliation in the Middle East. We work for peace in a threatened world."

POLITICAL AFFILIATION: Fellowship of Reconciliation.

RELIGIOUS AFFILIATION: Jewish.

FOCUS: Global • Middle East. Human rights • militarism, peace, disarmament • nuclear arms and energy • international awareness • conscientious objection.

ACTIVITIES: Popular education • political action • solidarity work • constituency education • legislative action • publishing • distribution of print matter • distribution of audiovisuals • overseas project support • draft counseling.

RESOURCES: Speakers • publications list • audiovisuals • books and literature.

PERIODICAL: *Shalom Newsletter.*

Middle East Institute, 1761 N St., NW, Washington, DC 20036. Tel: (202) 785-1141.

"The Middle East Institute, a non-profit corporation founded in 1946, strives to foster American understanding of the Middle East through lectures, conferences, panels, educational courses, publications, the George Camp Keiser Library, the Sultan Qaboos bin Said Research Center, its Islamic Affairs Program, Middle Eastern language program, and other activities. The institute serves as a resource center for objective information and discussion on contemporary developments in a diverse region of the world, takes no institutional position on the many controversies endemic to the Middle East and may neither by charter or tradition become the instrument of anyone's policy nor seek to influence legislation."

FOCUS: Middle East. Political economy • militarism, peace, disarmament • foreign aid and trade.

ACTIVITIES: Political action • research and writing • training of interns • constituency education • library services • dissemination of documentation and information • publishing • workshops and seminars.

RESOURCES: Speakers • audiovisuals • research services • curriculum guides • list of publications • books and literature • consultant services • library.

PERIODICAL: *The Middle East Journal.*

Middle East Outreach Council, Middle East Center, University of Utah, Salt Lake City, UT 84112. Tel: (801) 581-6181.

"Established in 1981 as a non-profit organization, MEOC focuses on increasing public knowledge about the lands, cultures, and peoples of the Middle East — from Morocco to Afghanistan — with emphasis on secondary education. Serving no political causes, MEOC disseminates factual information to correct inaccuracies and to dispel myths and stereotypes by (1) sponsoring or collaborating on seminars and workshops for educators, business leaders, and the general public; (2) developing innovative educational materials; and (3) networking the Middle East Outreach Centers throughout the United States with other organizations and specialists affiliated with MEOC."

FOCUS: Middle East. Human rights • militarism, peace, disarmament • foreign aid and trade • women • political economy • international awareness • native peoples • food, hunger, agribusiness.

ACTIVITIES: Popular education • training of interns • distribution of print matter • production of audiovisuals • distribution of audiovisuals • workshops and seminars • overseas project support • foreign service.

RESOURCES: Speakers • audiovisuals • research services • curriculum guides • books and literature • consultant services • library.

PERIODICAL: *Middle East Center Newsletter.* 3 issues/year. Free with membership of $10/year.

Middle East Research and Information Project, 475 Riverside Dr., Rm. 518, New York, NY 10115. Tel: (212) 870-3281.

"For more than fifteen years, the Middle East Research and Information Project has been providing information on political struggles and economic developments in the Middle East. MERIP has a speakers' bureau that makes available articulate and knowledgeable persons who can discuss the critical issues relating to the Middle East and U.S. policy there. The staff of MERIP also responds to information requests from researchers and journalists, grants interviews for radio and television, and undertakes contract research."

FOCUS: Middle East. Political repression • militarism, peace, disarmament • foreign aid and trade • political economy • national liberation struggles • social justice • socialism.

ACTIVITIES: Popular education • research and writing • dissemination of documentation and information.

RESOURCES: Speakers • books and literature • library • reports.

PERIODICAL: *MERIP Middle East Report.*

Najda: Women Concerned about the Middle East, P.O. Box 7152, Berkeley, CA 94707.

"The year 1960 saw the final stages of the Algerian war of independence and the birth of 'Najda,' an Arabic word meaning 'assistance in time of need.' Today the organization that adopted the name Najda continues to provide medical and financial aid to the Arab world. At the same time, Najda attempts to promote understanding between Arabs and Americans by sponsoring and participating in community activities and monthly programs and by publishing and distributing printed materials."

FOCUS: Middle East. Human rights • women • international awareness • national liberation struggles • social justice • food, hunger, agribusiness.

ACTIVITIES: Popular education • political action • research and writing • solidarity work • networking • constituency education • library services • press service • dissemination of documentation and information • publishing • distribution of print matter • workshops and seminars • overseas project support.

RESOURCES: Speakers • audiovisuals • curriculum guides • books and literature • consultant services.

PERIODICAL: *Najda Newsletter.* 6 issues/year. Free with membership of $5/year.

New Jewish Agenda, 64 Fulton St., Rm. 1100, New York, NY 10038. Tel: (212) 227–5885.

"New Jewish Agenda was founded in December 1980 and now has offices in New York and Los Angeles and chapters in more than forty U.S. cities. NJA's 5,000 members work for peace and social justice by applying Jewish religious and secular history and values to local organizing on current domestic and international concerns. Priority issues include peace and justice in the Middle East and Central America, feminism, disarmament, economic and social justice, lesbian and gay rights, and opposition to racism, anti-Semitism, and apartheid."

FOCUS: Middle East • Israel. Human rights • militarism, peace, disarmament • nuclear arms and energy • women • political economy • social justice.

ACTIVITIES: Popular education • political action • research and writing • solidarity work • media relations • networking • policy-oriented research and writing • workshops and seminars.

RESOURCES: Speakers • audiovisuals • books and literature.

PERIODICAL: *Agenda Newsletter*. 4 issues/year.

November 29th Committee for Palestine, P.O. Box 27462, San Francisco, CA 94127. Tel: (415) 861–1552.

"The November 29th Committee for Palestine takes its name from the date declared by the United Nations as the International Day of Solidarity with the Palestinian People. Our task is to spark and support consistent, far-reaching, and effective activity which brings the issue of Palestine before the American people and builds a growing and deepening base of understanding. Our committee organizes to stop U.S. intervention in the Middle East and to cut off U.S. aid to Israel. We educate Americans on the need to support the Palestine Liberation Organization, which is the sole legitimate representative of the Palestinian people, and to oppose Israeli policies of discrimination which deny the Palestinian people their rights."

FOCUS: Middle East. Human rights of Palestinians • militarism, peace, disarmament • social justice • U.S. aid to Israel • Palestine Liberation Organization.

ACTIVITIES: Popular education • political action • dissemination of documentation and information • publishing.

RESOURCES: Publications • speakers.

PERIODICAL: *Palestine Focus*.

Palestine Human Rights Campaign, 220 S. State St., One Quincy Ct., Suite 1308, Chicago, IL 60604. Tel: (312) 987–1995.

"Established in 1977 to secure internationally recognized human rights for the Palestinian people, the PHRC investigates and documents abuses of Palestinian rights, lending all possible support to those whose rights have been violated. Composed of individuals drawn from religious, academic, civil rights, and peace communities, the campaign has local chapters and affiliates throughout the United States and Canada. Membership is open to all concerned with securing universal rights by defending the individual, institutional, and national rights of the Palestinian people."

FOCUS: Middle East. Human rights • militarism, peace, disarmament • social justice • political repression • education.

ACTIVITIES: Popular education • political action • media relations • networking • policy-oriented research and writing • dissemination of documentation and information • publishing • workshops and seminars.

RESOURCES: Speakers • books and literature • consultant services.

PERIODICAL: *Palestine Human Rights Newsletter*.

Palestine Research and Educational Center, 2025 Eye St., NW, Suite 415, Washington, DC 20006. Tel: (202) 466–3205.

"The Palestine Research and Educational Center was incorporated in Washington, D.C., on 30 November 1983 as an independent, non-profit educational institution specializing in Palestinian affairs. Through research, publication, and other educational programs, the center seeks to provide information about the Palestinian people, their history, society, culture, and institutions."

FOCUS: International • Middle East. Human rights • militarism, peace, disarmament • international awareness • life under military occupation.

ACTIVITIES: Popular education • research and writing • media relations • constituency education • Congressional testimony • library services • dissemination of documentation and information.

RESOURCES: Speakers • research services • books and literature • consultant services • computerized data bank • occasional papers • library.

PERIODICAL: *Palestine Perspectives.*

Resource Center for Nonviolence, Middle East Program, 515 Broadway, Santa Cruz, CA 95060. Tel: (408) 423-1626.

"The Middle East Program of the Resource Center for Nonviolence has developed in five related areas: (1) conducting educational programs, such as our Middle East Peace Delegations/Study Tours, conferences, forums, and study groups; (2) initiating and organizing national speaking tours and hosting speakers from the Middle East; (3) producing written resources and publishing articles in a variety of publications; (4) collaborating with various U.S. organizations concerned with Middle East peace and with a special commitment to putting the Arab/Israeli conflict on the agenda of the U.S. peace movement and social justice groups; and (5) establishing and cultivating personal contacts and cooperation with individuals who generally share our point of view or reflect our values in their approach to Middle East concerns."

FOCUS: Middle East. Nonviolent methods of peacemaking • human rights • labor • women • international awareness • social justice • development.

ACTIVITIES: Study tours to the Middle East • popular education • research and writing • media relations • networking • library services • dissemination of documentation and information • workshops and seminars.

SUPPLEMENTARY LIST OF ORGANIZATIONS

MIDDLE EAST

Americans for Justice in the Middle East, P.O. Box 113-5581, Beirut, Lebanon.
Arab Studies Society, Orient House Bldg., 10 Abu Obeida Ibn Al-Jarah St., P.O. Box 20479, Jerusalem 281012, Israel.
General Arab Women Federation, Hay Al-Maghreb, Mahaela 304, Zuqaq 5/33, Baghdad, Iraq.
Women against the Occupation, P.O. Box 2760, Tel Aviv, Israel.

CANADA

Canadian Arab Federation, 5298 Dundas St. West, Islington, Ontario M9B 1B2, Canada. Tel: (416) 231-7524.
Canadian Friends of Peace Now, P.O. Box 76, Sta. Z, Toronto, Ontario M5N 1AO, Canada.
Near East Cultural and Educational Foundation of Canada, 106 Duplex Ave., Toronto, Ontario M5P 2A7, Canada. Tel: (416) 483-6467.
Le Regroupement pour un Dialogue Israel-Palestine, P.O. Box 47, Sta. Victoria, Montreal, Quebec H32 2V4, Canada.

EUROPE

British Anti-Zionist Organization, Palestine Solidarity, c/o Dr. G. Mitchell, 90 John St., Glasgow, Scotland.
Council for the Advancement of Arab-British Understanding, Arab-British Centre, 21 Collingham Rd., London SW5 0NU, England.
International Centre for Information on Palestinian and Lebanese Prisoners, Centre International d'Information sur le Droit Humanitaire, B.P. 355.16, Paris Cedex 16 F-75767, France.
United Nations Committee on the Exercise of the Inalienable Rights of the Palestinian People, Palais des Nations, CH-1211 Geneva, Switzerland. Or United Nations, New York, NY 10017.
United Nations Special Committee to Investigate Israeli Practices Affecting the Human Rights of the Occupied Territories. Palais des Nations, CH-1211 Geneva, Switzerland. Or United Nations, New York, NY 10017.

UNITED STATES

America-Israel Friendship League, 134 E. 39 St., New York, NY 10016. Tel: (212) 679-4822.
America-Mideast Educational and Training Services, 1100 17 St., NW, Washington, DC 20036. Tel: (202) 785-0022.

American Educational Trust, P.O. Box 53062, Washington, DC 20009. Tel: (202) 939–6050.

American Institute of Iranian Studies, University of Pennsylvania, 325 University Museum, Philadelphia, PA 19104.

American Jewish Committee, 165 E. 56 St., New York, NY 10022. Tel: (212) 751–4000.

American Middle East Peace Research Institute, P.O. Box 524, Prudential Center, Boston, MA 02199. Tel: (617) 266–5568.

American Near East Refugee Aid, 1522 K St., NW, Suite 202, Washington, DC 20005. Tel: (202) 347–2558.

American-Arab Affairs Council, 1730 M St., NW, Suite 512, Washington, DC 20036. Tel: (202) 296–6767.

American-Arab Relations Committee, 820 Second Ave., Rm. 302, New York, NY 10017. Tel: (212) 682–1154.

Anti-Defamation League of B'nai B'rith, 823 UN Plaza, New York, NY 10017. Tel: (212) 490–2525.

Arab People to American People, 820 Second Ave., Suite 302, New York, NY 10017. Tel: (212) 972–0460.

Arab-American Media Society, Penobscot Bldg., Suite 1450, Detroit, MI 48226. Tel: (313) 882–9693.

Attiyeh Foundation, 3808 Reno Rd., NW, Washington, DC 20008. Tel: (202) 966–8765.

Campaign for Peace with Justice in the Middle East, c/o American Friends Service Committee, 2161 Massachusetts Ave., Cambridge, MA 02140. Tel: (617) 661–6130.

Committee for Academic Freedom in the Israeli Occupied Territories, 300 Eshelman Hall, University of California, Berkeley, CA 94720.

Duncan Black MacDonald Center for the Study of Islam and Christian-Muslim Relations, Hartford Seminary, 77 Sherman St., Hartford, CT 06105. Tel: (203) 232–4451.

Foundation for Middle East Peace, 555 13 St., NW, Washington, DC 20004. Tel: (202) 637–6557.

Friends of Peace Now (USA), 27 W. 20 St., 9th floor, New York, NY 10011.

Institute of Turkish Studies, 2010 Massachusetts Ave., NW, Washington, DC 20036. Tel: (202) 296–4502.

International Jewish Peace Union, P.O. Box 5672, Berkeley, CA 94705.

Interns for Peace, 270 W. 89 St., New York, NY 10024.

Jerusalem Fund, 2435 Virginia Ave., NW, Washington, DC 20037. Tel: (202) 338–1958.

Middle East Librarians' Association, Ohio State University, Main Library, Rm. 310, 1858 Neil Avenue Mall, Columbus, OH 43210. Tel: (614) 422–8389.

National Association of Arab Americans, 2033 M St., NW, 9th floor, Washington, DC 20036. Tel: (202) 467–4800.

National Committee for Middle East Studies in Secondary Education, 330 Seventh Ave., New York, NY 10016. Tel: (212) 563–2580.

National Council on U.S.-Arab Relations, 1625 Eye St., NW, Washington, DC 20006. Tel: (202) 293-0801.

North American Friends of Palestinian Universities, 51 Prentiss St., Rm. 2, Cambridge, MA 02140.

Palestine Aid Society, 1051 Penobscot Bldg., Detroit, MI 48226. Tel: (313) 961-7252.

Palestine Congress of North America, 4401 East-West Highway, Bethesda, MD 20814. Tel: (301) 652-0052.

Palestine Information Office, 818 18 St., NW, Suite 620, Washington, DC 20006. Tel: (202) 466-3348.

Washington Area Jews for an Israeli Palestinian Peace, 17814 Buhlr Rd., Olney, MD 20832. Tel: (301) 774-0832.

INFORMATION SOURCES

The organizations included in this directory are for the most part regionally focused. Organizations such as Amnesty International, Clergy and Laity Concerned, and the Data Center are not included because their interests and resources are broader than this one region. These organizations do, however, include the Middle East region in the course of their educational programs and information gathering and they should, therefore, be contacted. For information on such groups, see the bibliographies, guides, and reference books described in chapter 2 below.

The spring 1987 issue of *Third World Resources* listed and described numerous reference guides that contain information on Middle East-related organizations, such as the *Directory of Non-Governmental*

Organizations for Rural Development (U.N. Food and Agriculture Organization), *The New Global Yellow Pages* (Global Perspectives in Education), and the excellent series of directories from Human Rights Internet. Copies of the spring 1987 issue of *Third World Resources* are available from the publishers for 50 cents (464 19 St., Oakland, CA 94612). For a list of other Third World Resources publications, see the preface to this resource directory.

The **New Israel Fund** has published *A Guide to Arab-Jewish Peacemaking in Israel* (June 1984. 41pp. $3), edited by Jay Rothman and Sharon Bray, that contains annotated lists of "human relations organizations" and "research, policy, and political organizations" in Israel. All of the groups in the directory "work toward peace in various ways," the editors explain. Some of the organizations work on the interpersonal level; others seek to influence public institutions; and still others strive to build peace "by overcoming economic and political inequalities between Israeli Jews and Arabs."

The May/June 1986 issue of *New Outlook* magazine contained a five-page annotated listing (pp. 67–71) of Israeli movements and institutions concerned with peace and coexistence. The list included extraparliamentary peace movements; educational, cultural, and community groups; civil rights groups; research and policy institutes; academic institutions; nonviolent activist groups; internationally oriented activist groups; political parties; cultural activist groups; and "Palestinian connections." In the latter category the editors of *New Outlook* note that in 1986 the *Al-Fajr* English-language newspaper (see chapter 3 below) published a comprehensive list of addresses, telephone numbers, and contacts of Palestinian institutions in the West Bank, the Gaza Strip, and East Jerusalem. Write the main office of *Al-Fajr* for information: 2 Hatem al-Ta'ee St., P.O. Box 20517, Jerusalem. Tel: (02) 281035.

See also the publications from **Third World Resources** described in the preface to this resource directory.

2

Books

This chapter is divided into three parts: annotated entries, supplementary list of books, and sources of additional information on books related to the Middle East.

The part called **annotated entries** is divided into five sections: general; bibliographies; catalogs, directories, guides; study guides and curriculum materials; and reference books. Information in the annotated entries is given in the following order: author(s) or editor(s); title; place of publication; publisher; date of publication; number of pages; price; keyword description of format; description of content.

Books in the **supplementary list** (pp. 45–52) are grouped under these headings: Middle East general (with subheadings for foreign relations; Islam; Arab-Israeli relations; oil; and women); Arabian Peninsula and Gulf; Fertile Crescent (with subheadings for Israel and the Jews; Jordan; Lebanon; Palestine and the Palestinians; and the Occupied Territories); Iran; and Iraq. Information in the entries in this section is given in the following order: author(s) or editor(s); title; place of publication; publisher; date of publication; number of pages.

The part entitled **information sources** (p. 52) provides the names of directories and guides that contain the titles of other books related to the Middle East.

All titles are integrated into the titles index at the back of the directory. The addresses for most of the publishers and distributors appear in the organizations index. (We have omitted addresses when we judged that a particular book could be easily acquired through a bookstore or library.) We have given the North American distributors for books published outside the United States. Readers in other countries should check with publishers for local distributors. All Zed books are available in North America from Humanities Press, Atlantic Highlands, NJ 07716.

Americans for Middle East Understanding (AMEU) offers generous discounts on many of the titles in this section. Write for their annual catalog.

All books are paperback unless we indicate that they are clothbound.

ANNOTATED ENTRIES

General

American Friends Service Committee. *A Compassionate Peace: A Future for the Middle East.* **New York and Toronto: Hill and Wang, 1982. 226pp. $6.95. Maps, notes, documents, bibliography, appendixes.**

This AFSC report was compiled and written by a working party composed of five scholars and activists — all of them North Americans. The authors admit to their biases from the start: "This report is frankly biased and unashamedly visionary," they declare. "It is biased toward people and against arms, toward peace and against strife and suffering, toward justice and against fear and insecurity. It is visionary because we believe, in spite of all the difficulties and setbacks, that peace, justice, and security can be achieved in the Middle East." It speaks volumes about the contentious situation in the Middle East today that there are those who would take issue with this lofty AFSC position, accusing the American Friends Service Committee of being dupes of the Palestine Liberation Organization and so forth.

AFSC brings to its quest for a "compassionate peace" long years of involvement in the Middle East, dating back to its work during and after World War II with Jewish and non-Jewish refugees. AFSC workers have been — and *are* — there, in the field, with the people. They speak and write from this perspective. Their report, *A Compassionate Peace,* brings this wealth of personal experience to bear on issues as wide-ranging as terrorism, designs for a transition to an independent Palestinian state, nuclear weapons in the Middle East, the 1979 Soviet invasion of Afghanistan, the U.S. response to the Iranian revolution, the Camp David Accord, and much more.

The authors acknowledge the fact that "no one from outside can save the nations of the Middle East from themselves," but they do look to the United States to play "a catalytic role in bringing the conflicting parties together to confront and resolve the most intractable issues."

AFSC's level-headed, knowledgeable, and optimistic approach to issues of war and peace in the Middle East makes this report highly recommended for an introduction to the region.

Atiya, Nayra. *Khul-Khaal: Five Egyptian Women Tell Their Stories.* **Syracuse, N.Y.: Syracuse University Press, 1982. 216pp. $11.95. Photographs.**

U.S.-educated writer, poet, and painter Nayra Atiya has gathered oral histories from five Egyptian women who share much in common: they all reside in an urban environment; they are all in one way or another attempting to survive "in the monied economy of city life"; all but one come from the lower social class; and all but one never received more than a primary school education.

"The women have in common," Atiya adds, "their extraordinary natural perception about the world in which we live. The stories provide us with a rich mine of materials on which to reflect — these are not specially talented storytellers — rather they have absorbed the narrative skills that are particularly developed among the folk of Egypt. When we listen to the women talking about their lives, we get a sense that they have brooded a great deal over their destinies. There is a philosophical breadth and eloquence to the narratives — a richness of expression — that one might not expect in people of such substandard physical environments. These women are philosophers."

Atiya characterizes the stories she collected in these words: "Better than analytical models, these stories give the meaning of kinship structures, decision-making vectors, cultural symbols, systems of obligations and rights, and of economic and social adaptation to particular environments. They show concepts, world view, domestic cycle regularities, and values and norms without the technical terms that reduce these processes to cold and formal dimensions."

The stories in *Khul-Khaal* present an unsettling challenge to Westerners, who, Atiya believes, "have come too quickly to expect that ours are the international expectations of feminism — that other women will come to want the same rights and goals we seek — or, that once a society is frankly dominated in certain spheres by men, women will be a suppressed and passive group." "Nothing could be further from the truth," Atiya concludes, "as the pages of this book indicate. What is important to understand is how such seeming contradictions by western standards can be reconciled into a way of life that is both consistent and fulfilling to a large portion of Egyptians, male and female."

The *khul-khaal* of the book's title are heavy silver or gold anklets worn by married women. Atiya explains that though they resemble shackles, they can also be used to advantage — as items that can be sold in times of extreme need or can be used to call attention seductively to the wearer.

Bendt, Ingela, and James Downing. *We Shall Return: Women of Palestine.* **Trans. Ann Henning. London: Zed Books, 1982. 144pp. $8.50. Available in North America from Humanities Press. Map, tables, photographs, chronology.**

This on-site investigation of the situation of Palestinian women in Lebanon by two freelance journalists from Sweden met with two responses. The first, from a headmaster in the village of Souk al Gharb: "For you, in the West, women's circumstances are a luxury to investigate; here we're fighting for our lives!" The second, from a young woman in the Palestinian Women's Association: "It's about time. . . . All the time we are the ones who sacrifice and suffer the most. . . . The woman carries two-thirds of the social responsibility; the man carries the rest."

Bendt and Downing offer a moving portrait of Palestinian women — their day-to-day struggles in Lebanon's refugee camps and their efforts to create a homeland for the Palestinian people. As if in response to one Palestinian woman's dismay that foreigners want "to give *their* picture of events, not ours," *We Shall Return* lets the women speak for themselves.

Um Leila, one of the last women the authors interviewed before leaving Lebanon, captured the steadfast dedication of the Palestinian women: "One final thing, one thing you must mention in your book. Write that in spite of all the obstacles, in spite of war and death, in spite of the opposition from the men, the Palestinian women will participate in the liberation struggle. . . . Without the women the Revolution would be without a future."

Berberoglu, Berch. *Turkey in Crisis: From State Capitalism to Neocolonialism.* **London: Zed Books, 1982. 150pp. $9.95. Available in North America from Humanities Press. Map, figures, tables, bibliography, index.**

The author's opening statement about the focus of *Turkey in Crisis* should be sufficient to warn off those who might be looking for an easy-reading introduction to this little-known country. "This book," Berberoglu states, "is a study in the political economy of state capitalism in the Third World as applied to the case of Turkey. It examines the Turkish case as a classic example of a post-The Great Depression state capitalist formation in the Third World during the second quarter of this century and traces its transformation into a neo-colonial state in the period since World War II."

Berberoglu's work is obviously written for the serious student of political economy. He uses the Turkish experience to demonstrate "the long-term impossibility of independent, national state capitalist development in the Third World." Turkey's rulers, Berberoglu shows, have so undermined the country's capacity for social and economic development that it is now incapable of providing full employment and rising living standards for its people, let alone democratic government and rights for its national minorities. Turkey's fate, the author concludes, contains serious lessons for other Third World countries. A capitalist path of development led by the state is no longer historically possible and a process of growth dependent on Western multinational corporations cannot meet the basic needs of the majority. Only through socialism, Berberoglu contends, "can imperialism be expelled and capitalism abolished."

For the most part Berberoglu builds his case effectively. At times, however, he lapses into rhetoric that will turn off both scholar and general reader (e.g., "Everywhere people are voicing their opposition to military rule, and are seeking answers beyond bourgeois democracy, and toward socialism").

The strategic political and military importance of Turkey and the suffering of the Turkish people under a brutal military regime are more than enough reasons for those in the West to care about the course of this country's development. Authors who set out to write a book on these vital subjects for the general reader would do well to avail themselves of Dr. Berberoglu's scholarship and political acumen.

Chomsky, Noam. *The Fateful Triangle: The United States, Israel and the Palestinians.* **Boston: South End Press, 1983. 481pp. $10. AMEU price: $7.95. Notes, index.**

MIT professor Noam Chomsky's opening chapter is entitled "Fanning the Flames." Those familiar with Chomsky's writings and speeches on current affairs know that he can always be counted on to do just that: fan the flames. He is relentless and uncompromising in his search for truth — in this case about the nature of the "the fateful triangle." References to newspapers, research reports, and journals on virtually every page of *The Fateful Triangle* testify to the fact that Chomsky reads voraciously. He reads with a critical eye as well. Books such as this challenge both those who rally to Chomsky's side and those who stand in opposition to his strong political viewpoints to read as widely and as critically as Chomsky himself does. Readers who allow Chomsky to fan the flames of their political awareness will find themselves much more attentive to the television news reports and the daily newspapers that too often simply wash over us.

In chapter 1 of *The Fateful Triangle* Chomsky explores the character and historical development of U.S. support for Israel and describes the effect that this special relationship has had on the Palestinian people. Chapter 2 defines the "special relationship" and searches for its origins in U.S. domestic pressure groups, U.S. strategic interests in the Middle East, and in American liberalism. Chapter 3 builds a framework for discussion of the status of Israel and the rival claims of the Palestinian people. The positions of the four major actors are studied: the United States, Israel, the population of the Occupied Territories, and the Arab States and the Palestine Liberation Organization. Chapters 4 and 5 treat the history of relations between the Arab and Israeli peoples in the region culminating in Israel's 1982 invasion of Lebanon. The concluding two chapters describe the aftermath of Israel's "Peace for Galilee" military operation and speculate about the course of future developments in the area.

The Fateful Triangle is disturbing — but necessary — reading on the critical issue of a just peace in the Middle East.

Cobban, Helena. *The Palestinian Liberation Organisation: People, Power, and Politics.* **New York: Cambridge University Press, 1984. 305pp. $8.95. AMEU price: $6.50. Notes, illustrations, figures, maps, references, bibliography, documents, appendixes.**

The fact that in the 1980s "the Palestinian question" remains on the world's agenda is — according to this study — testimony to the incredible strength of the Palestinian resistance movement. Against overwhelming odds, the movement has succeeded in affirming the Palestinian-ness of a people whose native home was literally eliminated from maps and books. "In the 50's," Cobban quotes Yassir Arafat as saying in 1979, "John Foster Dulles used to say that the new generation of Palestinians would not even know Palestine. But they did! The group that made the [March 1978] operation against Israel were nearly all of them born outside Palestine, but they were prepared to die for it."

Helena Cobban draws on five years of experience as a journalist in Beirut (1976-81) and on documentary sources never before included in Western analyses to explain the success of the Palestinian resistance movement in the face of opposition not only from Israel but also—at times—from the wider Arab community.

The Palestinian Liberation Organisation opens with the PLO in the 1980s—in the wake of the Israeli invasion of Lebanon in 1982—and then jumps back to 1948 to trace the development of the "PLO mainstream" (the PLO itself and its dominant member-group, Fateh). This historical section spans the years 1948-1983.

The remaining two sections of *The Palestinian Liberation Organisation* treat the PLO's *internal* relations (with the non-Fateh guerrilla groups and with the 1.2 million Palestinians who live within the boundaries of historic Palestine) and the movement's *external* relations (with the Arab states and with the international community).

The book closes with a discussion of the "irresistible force" (Palestinian nationalism) and the "immovable object" (U.S. policy).

Committee against Repression and for Democratic Rights in Iraq (CARDRI). *Saddam's Iraq: Revolution or Reaction?* **London: Zed Press, 1985. 272pp. $9.95. Available in North America from Humanities Press. Maps, references, bibliography, chronology, index.**

This collection of essays by Iraqi and British academics and political activists traces the political history of Iraq from the late nineteenth century, when it was three Ottoman provinces, to late 1984. Articles cover the administration and policies of the government of President Saddam Husain, the conditions of the Iraqi people, oil and the Iraqi economy, the problems of Iraq's Kurdish minority, women in Iraq, political repression and torture, and the causes of the Gulf War with Iran.

Reports of terror and repression in Iraq in late 1978 led many British parliamentarians and others to sponsor the formation of CARDRI, with the aim of exposing "the brutality of the Ba'th regime and developing solidarity with those in Iraq struggling for human and democratic rights in immensely difficult and dangerous conditions." *Saddam's Iraq* is CARDRI's attempt to enlist the informed involvement of others in their noble cause.

EAFORD & AJAZ. *Judaism or Zionism? What Difference for the Middle East?* **London: Zed Press, 1985. 320pp. $12.25. Available in North America from Humanities Press. AMEU price: $8.95. Notes, documentation, index, appendixes.**

More than twenty specialists in theology, politics, international law, history, and journalism examine here the problems created by political Zionism for Jews and Judaism, as well as for Palestine and Palestinians and the Middle East as a whole. In the process they aim to drive home the point that Zionism and Judaism are *not* synonymous. In fact, the editors maintain, ". . . only a minority of American Jews are card-carrying Zionists." And, they explain, "There is a long, historic tradition of rejection of political/national Zionism, not only in the United States, but in all democratic states."

At the invitation of two nongovernmental organizations, American Jewish Alternatives to Zionism (AJAZ) and the International Organization for the Elimination of All Forms of Racial Discrimination (EAFORD), scholars from the United States, Europe, and the Middle East, and from three religious traditions (Judaism, Christianity, and Islam) met in Washington, D.C., in May 1983 to voice their grave doubts about the possibility of any genuine peace while Israel remains committed to the militant exclusivism of political Zionism. At the same time, they affirmed their support for the full self-determination for the Palestinian people and the right of the Jews to live in dignity and equality wherever they may be.

The more than sixteen papers, statements, messages, and other remarks are divided into four sections: (1) What did God promise? A look at the Scriptures; (2) Cultural dimensions of Zionism; (3) International aspects of Zionism; and (4) Zionism: Help or hindrance to U.S. foreign policy?

Farhang, Mansour. *U.S. Imperialism: The Spanish American War to the Iranian Revolution.* **Boston: South End Press, 1981. 250pp. $7. Notes, bibliography, index.**

This historical study of U.S. imperialism has a number of virtues to recommend it. It is written by a man who combines academic scholarship with a passionate engagement in the revolutionary process in his native Iran. It is popular and conversational in tone, making it easy reading. And it joins an exposition of political theory with concrete examples of U.S. policies in the Middle East and in Iran.

After a lengthy foreword and introduction by Princeton University's Richard Falk, Farhang opens his study with a chapter devoted to an exposition of the "evolving theories of imperialism." In the following chapter he attempts to go "beneath and beyond the Marxist and liberal theories of imperialism" and to understand U.S. imperialism as "a transnational system of privilege." "Transnationalism," Farhang explains, "represents the ability of the privileged few in two or more nation-states to join forces across national boundaries and together confront the revolutionary challenge from below in the subordinated society. At the same time," he continues, "this transnational system of privilege allows the dominant countries to pacify the domestic opposition by making possible a higher standard of living and providing the benefits of welfare capitalism."

The remainder of *U.S. Imperialism* is given to an historical study of how the economic, political, military, and ideological dimensions of U.S. imperialism developed from the time of the Spanish-American War (1898) through the Iranian revolution of the late 1970s. Farhang's concluding chapter assesses the future of imperialism and "the struggle for a humane world."

Fernea, Elizabeth Warnock, and Basima Qattan Bezirgan, eds. *Middle Eastern Muslim Women Speak.* **Austin: University of Texas Press, 1977. 402pp. $11.50. Map, illustrations, photographs.**

Muhsin Mahdi's foreword points out the "false notion that the world of Islam is a world created by men for men rather than a joint creation of men and women" and suggests that neither the men nor the women of the Middle Eastern Muslim culture are perfectly understood. The editors of this work try to further some of this understanding by presenting a "direct view of the world of Middle Eastern Muslim women as seen by these women themselves."

The book is a classic collection of writings and documents by and about Muslim women. The women whose lives and works are represented here come from differing classes, occupations, and perspectives. The selections are arranged chronologically, beginning with quotations from the Koran (A.D. 600–670) and ending with a discussion on Future Directions by an Egyptian feminist, Aminah al-Sa'id (b. 1914). The editors precede each selection with a brief introduction. Many of the selections are printed here in English for the first time.

Is the Middle Eastern woman held in bondage by her society or is she an effective agent helping to form that society? The editors suggest in their long and informative introduction to the book that the real situation is in neither position but lies instead somewhere between the two.

"The only way to get a fresh view through the kaleidoscope of Middle Eastern society and to combat the stereotyped thinking of the past is to go back to the primary sources, the multicolored shapes within the instrument, and let Middle Eastern women speak for themselves." The editors have accomplished their aim and have provided us with a much-needed means of getting beyond "stereotyped thinking." Although the book was published in 1977, it is still timely and extremely useful toward furthering understanding of Muslim women and Muslim culture of the Middle East.

Fernea, Elizabeth Warnock, and Robert A. Fernea. *The Arab World: Personal Encounters.* **Garden City, N.Y.: Anchor Press/Doubleday, 1985. 366pp. $19.95. Cloth. Photographs, index.**

The authors, whose names are synonymous with stimulating and accurate information on the Middle East, first went to that part of the world in 1956. Since then they have devoted their lives to learning about the region and its people and communicating what they have learned.

This book of "Personal Encounters" has been written out of the authors' "concern over the incomplete image, even stereotype, which Americans have of the Arabs and out of [their] concern with ongoing change which is affecting us in America as well as in the Arab world."

"To understand the nature of change," theFerneas write, "its effects on families and individuals, we must turn to the patterns of people's lives." They turn to their friends — old friends in Egypt, Iraq, Morocco, Lebanon, and new friends in Yemen, Jordan, Libya, and Saudi Arabia. Each chapter records, using dialogue and a story-telling style, meetings, encounters, with these old and new friends. Although these people do not represent all of this very diverse area, they authentically represent important parts of it in a most striking way.

Sometimes the scene is set twenty-five years back; we may re-meet these same persons in the same geographical location in the 1980s. The changes do not have to be elaborated upon. Following each chapter is a section called "Comment"; it serves to point out historical patterns and particular relevancies for North Americans.

The Arab World covers many facets of change in an attractive and readable manner: it addresses independence, oil-wealth, imported labor, refugees, industrialization, women, consumerism, civil wars, invasions, public education, unemployment, the media, religion. A personal but eminently instructive account of the Arab world.

Findley, Paul. *They Dare to Speak Out: People and Institutions Confront Israel's Lobby.* **Westport, Conn.: Lawrence Hill and Co., 1985. 362pp. $16.95. Notes, index.**

Paul Findley must have been doing something right. After serving as Congressional representative from Illinois for twenty-two years (1960–82), Findley was finally driven from Congress by the very political lobby whose inordinate political influence he had come to question and challenge: the American-Israel Public Affairs Committee (AIPAC).

In this courageous, eye-opening book, Findley sounds an alarm: "Israel, through the deep and pervasive power of its lobby [AIPAC], threatens deeply cherished American values — especially free speech, academic freedom and our commitment to human rights."

In a preface to the new edition (written July 4, 1986) the author describes "alarming happenings [that] give new urgency to the warnings expressed in this book." "Recent revelations," he explains, "make it painfully evident that [the Israeli government] spies on the United States, lies to our highest officials, corrupts our political process and undercuts our national security interests to suit its own purposes."

They Dare to Speak Out describes what happens to those who search for and publicize the truth about the enormous power that the Israeli government wields in Washington, D.C., and, indeed, throughout the United States. Findley writes about a broad range of people and institutions that have felt the wrath of AIPAC, from Noam Chomsky to *National Geographic* magazine, from Jesse Jackson to former U.S. ambassador to the United Nations George Ball.

Findley writes with color and passion — and with no holds barred. Educators whose responsibility it is to teach about the Middle East, activists who desire to work for peace and justice in that troubled part of the globe, and U.S. taxpayers who foot the bill for many of the Israeli government's less-than-honorable, activities should examine Findley's charges with careful concern.

Gadant, Monique, ed. *Women of the Mediterranean.* **Trans. A. M. Berrett. London: Zed Books, 1987. 196pp. $11.50. Available in North America from Humanities Press. Tables, notes.**

First published in French as a special issue of *Peuples Mediterraneens* in 1984, *Women of the Mediterranean* contains articles by nineteen contributors including an Algerian midwife, two Turkish social workers whose clients are immigrants, an Italian professor of anthropology, and an official of the Union of Palestinian Women.

Similarities among the women whose homelands touch the Mediterranean are not the point here, although these similarities are readily apparent to the reader. The editor instead wants to underline the differences — "the difference that separates the developed capitalist countries along the northern edge [of the Mediterranean] from the others (whether Christian or Moslem), those which have been left behind in industrial growth or were former colonies."

Many issues emerge: male emigration and female staying-behind, women's participation in national liberation struggles, women's position after liberation and after socialism (Algeria, Yugoslavia), Islamic fundamentalism as a support for women's liberation.

The atmosphere and reality of war in Lebanon, the life of the weavers in Algeria, the Iranian revolution — none can be fully understood without the firsthand descriptions of such women as those represented in this book. Accounts of women from Europe (Spain, Italy, and Yugoslavia) provide an interesting contrast to accounts of Arab women. The book contributes to bridge-building between Western and Third World women.

Green, Stephen. *Taking Sides: America's Secret Relations with a Militant Israel.* **New York: William Morrow, 1984. 370pp. $14.95. Cloth. AMEU price: $11.50. List of acronyms, documentation, notes, index, appendixes.**

In the course of his research for this provocative study of U.S.-Israeli relations Stephen Green filed more than one hundred Freedom of Information Act requests with twenty-two different government agencies and spent more than two years examining previously classified files in the National Archives and in several of the presidential libraries. Green admits that *Taking Sides* is not a history of the Middle East, nor even a history of U.S.-Israeli relations. "It is," he says, "a collection of historical vignettes that have been — and I freely acknowledge this — carefully selected."

Green gathered these vignettes with one aim in mind: "to bring into the public domain many hundreds of important documents and texts that, taken together, fill significant gaps in America's collective knowledge about our past relationship with Israel. Neither myths, disinformation, nor selective information constitute a healthy basis upon which to conduct our Middle East policy."

One example suffices to illustrate the truth of Green's contention: evidence presented throughout *Taking Sides* clearly and convincingly demonstrates that since 1946 Israel has had total military superiority over *all* the Arab states combined. For all the talk we hear of the Arabs threatening to "drive the Israelis into the sea" there is not one reputable U.S. military or intelligence estimate that substantiates such a capability.

This book makes fascinating reading. If read and heeded in the right places, it could even lead to a more honorable and enlightened relationship with the state of Israel.

Halevi, Ilan. *A History of the Jews: Ancient and Modern.* **Trans. A. M. Berrett. London: Zed Books, 1987. 258pp. $12.50. Available in North America from Humanities Press. Notes, index.**

Jewish author Ilan Halevi offers Jewish and non-Jewish readers alike an expansive and finely textured survey of the Jewish people from the time of Moses in the desert, through the Middle Ages, Europe, the "crisis" of World War II, Palestine, and finally to the creation of the state of Israel. Halevi's sweeping assessments of the history of the Jewish people appear to be scrupulously fair. He faces the hard questions—about Arabs as well as about Jews—and dismisses pat answers. *A History of the Jews* is an excellent one-volume presentation of more than two thousand years of colorful and controversial history.

Hiro, Dilip. *Iran under the Ayatollahs.* **London: Routledge & Kegan Paul, 1985. 416pp. $39.95. Cloth. Notes, glossary of Arabic and Persian words, list of abbreviations, Islamic calendars: lunar and solar, maps, bibliography, index.**

Journalist and author Dilip Hiro divides his study of Iran into three parts: (1) the rise of the Islamic state and the ascendancy of the Pahlavi dynasty; (2) the overthrow of the monarchy and the founding of the Islamic Republic under Ayatollah Khomeini; and (3) Iran's relations with the outside world (the Soviet bloc, the West, and the region). A conclusion and postscript bring Hiro's account up to mid-1984 and project the future course of Iran's Islamic revolution.

The longest section of *Iran under the Ayatollahs*—Part 2—opens with a description of the "explosion of freedom" that followed in the wake of the ouster of the Shah and then details the factional struggles that consumed the revolutionary forces that had cooperated in the overthrow of the monarchy: militant clerics, lay Islamic radicals, liberal secular forces, Marxist-Leninist groups, and others. Hiro describes and evaluates the rule of the Ayatollah Khomeini in level-headed and knowledgeable terms. He devotes a chapter each to the American hostage crisis and the Gulf War between Iran and Iraq—a brutal conflict that has proved to be the longest and bloodiest conventional warfare since the Second World War. Part 2 closes with an analysis of the guerrilla campaign waged by the Islamic regime's opponents, the Mujahedin.

Hiro brings scholarship and extensive personal experience in the region to this study of a sensitive and turbulent subject. The result is a concise, informed, and very readable account of the historical development of Islam and the nation of Iran during the last 500 years.

Dilip Hiro is also the author of *Inside the Middle East* (New York: McGraw-Hill, 1983).

Holden, David, and Richard Johns. *The House of Saud: The Rise and Rule of the Most Powerful Dynasty in the Arab World.* **New York: Holt, Rinehart and Winston, 1981. 569pp. $19.95. Cloth. Maps, photographs, notes, bibliography, index.**

It is difficult to avoid mind-boggling numbers when describing the House of Saud: Abdul Aziz Ibn Saud, to take just one example, fathered forty-five recorded sons by at least twenty-two different mothers representing most of the major Arabian tribes and families with whom it seemed prudent to form an alliance. (There were as many daughters from an even wider range of women, but, unfortunately, these family members do not figure largely in this tale.) Today the House of Saud numbers over four thousand people with some five hundred princes in direct line. British journalists Holden and Johns flesh out these numbers in this very colorful and dramatic description of the emergence of this dynasty from its desert origins in the early part of this century to its present-day command of more than half of O.P.E.C.'s total output of oil. Their lengthy tale is peopled by soldiers of fortune, diplomats, bankers, multinational oil executives, greedy landlords, spies, Arab statesmen, and member after member of the House of Saud.

For ten years before his mysterious assassination in a roadside ditch on the outskirts of Cairo in December 1977 David Holden had been the Chief Foreign Correspondent of *The Sunday Times* (London). Holden's first-person account covers the first ten chapters of this monumental account. Richard Johns, who was the Middle East editor of *The Financial Times* at the time of Holden's death, picked up where his friend left off and completed *The House of Saud* during the period 1978-81.

Jansen, Michael. *The Battle of Beirut*. Boston: South End Press, 1983. 142pp. $6.50. Maps, photographs, chronology.

Michael Jansen, a journalist who has reported on Middle Eastern affairs for more than twenty years, does not pretend in this book to write a complete history of "Israel's fifth war." She has instead produced a study of the effects of Israel's military movement north to Beirut on the citizens of Beirut and of southern Lebanon — Lebanese and Palestinians alike.

Jansen describes the military plan behind Israel's invasion in June 1982 and U.S. support for it. She went to Israel to discover and observe firsthand the effects of the war on Israeli opinion. She reports on the negative effects, the failure, of this "successful" military operation on the Israeli people.

The book is an indictment of Israel's actions in Lebanon. It is thoroughly documented from European, North American, and Israeli press reports.

Khalaf, Samir. *Lebanon's Predicament*. New York: Columbia University Press, 1987. 328pp. $30. Cloth. Notes, statistical tables, bibliography, index.

A prominent Lebanese sociologist, Samir Khalaf has brought together in this book twelve essays he wrote over the past fifteen years. Unifying the whole is the theme of the nature of the dialectics between tradition and modernity.

The first chapter is an amplification of the theoretical question "Under what circumstances do some of the persisting sociocultural patterns and values reinforce and when do they undermine processes of social change and development?" Khalaf puts forward the thesis that the very social and psychic factors that support and hold the Lebanese together at the local level often prevent their cooperation at the national level.

Chapters 2 and 3 provide a historical framework, highlighting Lebanon's "fragmented political culture." The next three chapters deal with Lebanon's political system and patronage. Chapters 7 and 8 are about industrial development and voluntary associations, "kinship networks and family loyalty," supportive of individual growth and of the building of welfare structures. Chapters 9 and 10 deal with the area of public policy and planning, showing the interplay between sociocultural values and public policy. The last two chapters present some of the consequences of a decade of civil unrest. Khalaf's personal feelings — understandably — emerge here, as he laments the violence, dehumanization, indifference, and the mood of futility and defeat he sees overwhelming liberals. "Alas," he writes, "the Lebanese never seem to learn from their history. Otherwise, history would not be repeating itself; and with such menacing consequences."

Khalif's essays take us to issues that underly recent news reports of violence and military and political intervention. His presentation is constructive and thought-provoking.

El-Khawas, Mohamed, and Samir Abed-Rabbo. *American Aid to Israel: Nature and Impact.* **Brattleboro, Vt.: Amana Books, 1984. 191pp. $8.95. AMEU price: $5.95. Statistical tables, documentation, diagrams, photographs, maps, notes, chronology, appendixes.**

In his foreword to this analysis of U.S. economic and military aid to the State of Israel, Rabbi Elmer Berger estimates that the amount of grants and loans involved is "in the neighborhood of $40 *billion* since 1949."

The authors devote one-third of their study to an analysis and assessment of this colossal amount of aid. Part 2 is a critical examination of the "uncompromising Zionism which governs Israel today" and what this means for the United States.

The final one-third of the book — the *uncensored* draft of a June 1983 U.S. Government Accounting Office report on U.S. aid to Israel — makes eye-opening reading for U.S. taxpayers. Censored from the published GAO study, for instance, were these two items: (1) "According to the CIA, Israeli expectations are that the United States will fund half of its defense budget." (2) Despite assurances from Israel that its 1982 invasion of Lebanon would not result in any increase in requests for U.S. aid, the GAO cites U.S. government reports as admitting "that the increased aid and better terms requested by Israel in its current aid submission include compensation for its losses during the Lebanon campaign."

Mansfield, Peter. *The Arabs.* **Harmondsworth: Penguin Books, 1985. 3rd ed. 527pp. $6.95. Map, notes, index.**

Historian and journalist Peter Mansfield sweeps across the social, political, and historical elements of the Arab world — from the pre-Islamic nomads of Arabia, the life of Muhammad and the rise of Arab power that followed, to the Western colonial period, the tragedy of Palestine, and the modern Arab renaissance.

In Part 2 of *The Arabs* the author proceeds country-by-country, presenting a synopsis of the history of each. He begins with the nations of the Gulf, and then treats Oman, Saudi Arabia, the People's Democratic Republic of Yemen, the Yemen Arab Republic, Syria, Lebanon, Iraq, Jordan, Sudan, Egypt, Libya, Tunisia, Algeria, and Morocco.

In two concluding chapters, Mansfield looks at "the Arabs today," first through Western eyes, and then through Arab eyes. He concludes this impressive and readable survey by stating his belief that "the Arabs have a unique opportunity to enhance the unity of mankind by acting as a link between Europe and the West and the peoples of Africa and Asia." For, as Mansfield so well illustrates in *The Arabs,* "In certain important respects, they belong to all of them."

Porch, Douglas. *The Conquest of Morocco.* **New York: Fromm International, 1986. 335pp. $11.95. Map, photographs, bibliography, index.**

The conquest of Morocco, "France's last great colonial enterprise," is here told in colorful detail. Douglas Porch describes, in popular style, Morocco's cultures, towns, and settlements of the early 1900s, meeting places of Islam and Christian. The exotic flavor of that time and those places comes through in Porch's writing, as do the important facts of Morocco's strategic position at the entrance to the Mediterranean, its relationship to the European powers of the time, and its place in military history as a "watershed," for "it saw the first systematic application of a strategy, central to any modern counterinsurgency operation, which has more recently been termed 'the struggle for hearts and minds.'"

France's struggle for control of Morocco lasted from 1844 to 1934; Porch studies only the period from 1903 to 1934, during which the major events of the conquest took place. He pays particular attention to certain key figures: for example, Hubert Lyautey, French colonialist, strategist, and eccentric.

The author has used documents and memoirs of the time that are mostly European; thus the book does not furnish a Moroccan perspective. The book is, however, a no less fascinating and easy-to-read account.

Rubenberg, Cheryl. *Israel and the American National Interest: A Critical Examination.* **Champaign: University of Illinois Press, 1986. 429pp. $24.95. AMEU price: $14.95. Notes, tables, index.**

Flying in the face of prevailing "wisdom" regarding U.S. support for Israel, Cheryl Rubenberg argues in this provocative study that the U.S.-Israeli partnership has severely damaged U.S. national interests—politically, economically, and militarily. Using information gathered from her research and from extensive travels in the region Rubenberg substantiates her controversial position and then asks why Washington has pursued such a policy for more than thirty-five years.

"In the final analysis," Rubenberg states, "the explanation for the extraordinary and contradictory union [between Israel and the United States] rests on two factors: (1) a perception, based on erroneous assumptions and a total misunderstanding of the complexities of the Arab world but that nevertheless acquired the legitimacy of absolute truth in dominant sectors of the American foreign policymaking elite, that saw

Israel serving as an extension of American power in the Middle East and a strategic asset to U.S. interests; and (2) the power of the pro-Israeli lobby in American domestic politics."

In the first six chapters, *Israel and the American National Interest* traces the development of the U.S.-Israeli partnership (from the 1947 partition through the Israeli invasion of Lebanon in 1982) and then closes with an entire chapter on the efforts of the Israeli lobby in the United States.

The author admits to being a convert to the just cause of the Arab and Palestinian people. And she acknowledges that her findings regarding the negative effects of the U.S.-Israeli alliance did not at all fill her with glee. Rubenberg was educated and socialized—as many of us were—to accept many anti-Arab and pro-Israeli myths. In this well-documented study she invites her readers to summon the courage to face the truths behind these myths.

Rumaihi, Muhammad. *Beyond Oil: Unity and Development in the Gulf.* Trans. James Dickins. London: Al Saqi Books, 1986. 156pp. £4.95. Distributed in North America by Humanities Press. Notes, tables, index.

"The Gulf is not oil," says Muhammad Rumaihi. "The Gulf is its people and its land. So it was before the discovery of oil, and so it will remain when the oil disappears. Oil is no more than a historical phase in this part of the Arab world—and a rather short one at that." The concepts "Arab" and "oil" are so wedded in our consciousness that Rumaihi's instruction is most necessary and welcome. Oil is key to life in the Gulf today, but what about tomorrow?

The author, a professor of sociology at Kuwait University and editor-in-chief of the Arabic weekly magazine *al-Arabi,* believes that the future of the people and land of the Gulf turns on two axes, namely, comprehensive development and unity. These are the themes he develops in this short book.

Comprehensive development, Rumaihi explains, involves economic, social, cultural, and political aspects. He details the effects that a commitment to this type of development would have on oil production and distribution today and he describes how this course of development would benefit the majority of people in the Gulf region in the future.

By "unity" Rumaihi means the unity of the Arab world on the large-scale and of the smaller Gulf states in particular. He describes previous attempts at cooperation and coordination of efforts among the Arab states, particularly the Gulf Co-operation Council founded in 1981.

The final chapters in *Beyond Oil* cover culture and cultural development, women, and citizens and immigrant workers.

Rumaihi offers a concise and readable history of the people of the oil-producing countries of the Arabian peninsula. His strong desire—as an author—to bring the people of this region to life is evident on every page of *Beyond Oil.*

Said, Edward W. *After the Last Sky: Palestinian Lives.* New York: Pantheon Books, 1986. 174pp. $14.95 AMEU price: $8.95. Photographs.

"In the West, particularly in the United States," writes Edward Said, "Palestinians are not so much a people as a pretext for a call to arms." The point of this book, he goes on, "is to engage this difficulty ['the problem of writing about and representing the Palestinians generally'], to deny the habitually simple, even harmful representations of Palestinians, and to replace them with something more capable of capturing the complex reality of their experience."

Said's thoughtful prose guides the reader/viewer through the display of Swiss photographer Jean Mohr's dramatic black-and-white pictures, describing lines, gestures, and shadings of subtle meaning. The United Nations sponsored Jean Mohr's photo-taking trip to the Near East in 1983 to create an exhibit to be shown in Geneva at the International Conference on the Question of Palestine.

The book—with its "interplay of text and photos, the mixture of genres, modes, sytles"—does not pretend to tell a cohesive story or to set forth a political statement. "Fragmentary forms of expression," Said feels, are the most appropriate expression of the Palestinian people.

Said, Edward W. *Covering Islam: How the Media and the Experts Determine How We See the Rest of the World.* New York: Pantheon Books, 1981. 186pp. $3.95. Notes, index.

Covering Islam is the third and last in a series of books undertaken by Said to "treat the modern relationship between the world of Islam, the Arabs, and the Orient on the one hand, and on the other the West, France, Britain, and in particular the United States." *Orientalism*, the first in the series, traces the relationship of these two worlds from the Napoleonic invasion of Egypt to the emergence of U.S. dominance after World War II; its theme is "the affiliation of knowledge with power." The second book, *The Question of Palestine*, examines "the Palestinian national struggle for self-determination." The subject of *Covering Islam* is two-fold: the oversimplified image of Islam in the West and the use to which that image is put there, especially in the United States.

The title of the book is purposely double in meaning. The author contends that and shows how Islam is reported but not revealed as reality—"covering up" versus "coverage." We read or hear the term "Islam" almost daily. It seems to us both mystery and menace. Often, says Said, it is "only what holds the West's oil reserves." "In no really significant way," he writes, "is there a direct correspondence between 'Islam' in common Western usage and the enormously varied life that goes on within the world of Islam."

Said believes deeply in the "existence of a critical sense," and expects that the critical reader *can* learn about the real Islam. His book is intended to "advance that goal."

Said cites many examples to illustrate his thesis. Chief among them is a comparison of European and U.S. coverage of the Iran story. It should be read not only as a case in itself but also with an eye to news coverage of events in Central America, Africa, and every other part of the world.

The work is an eye-opener and an encouragement for all of us to use our "critical sense" and seek out more accurate knowledge that will lead to more complete understanding both of ourselves and of those who are different from us.

El Saadawi, Nawal. *The Hidden Face of Eve: Women in the Arab World*. London: Zed Books, 1982. 224pp. $9.25. Available in North America from Humanities Press. References.

"There is no doubt," writes Nawal El Saadawi, "that to write about women in Arab society, especially if the author is herself a woman, is to tread on difficult and sensitive areas." So sensitive has it been for Nawal El Saadawi that Egyptian censors refused to allow her books to be published in her homeland and, after the 1972 publication of her first work of non-fiction, *Woman and Sex*, she was dismissed from her post as Egypt's Director of Public Health. She subsequently wrote several other books in Arabic. *The Hidden Face of Eve* is her first book to appear in English.

The book is a personal story, both the author's own and that of the many patients she has helped over the years of her medical practice. It contains many moving accounts of unjust treatment of girls and women. The Western reader is not allowed to assume a self-righteous posture, however. El Saadawi is steadfast in her assertion that "the oppression of women, the exploitation and social pressures to which they are exposed, are not characteristic of Arab or Middle Eastern societies, or countries of the 'Third World' alone. They constitute an integral part of the political, economic and cultural system, preponderant in most of the world." Islam is not to be blamed for women's oppression. "We the women in Arab countries realize that we are still slaves, still oppressed, not because we belong to the East, not because we are Arab, or members of Islamic societies, but as a result of the patriarchal class system that has dominated the world since thousands of years."

An afterword succinctly restates the main points Nawal El Saadawi wants to make: Islamic, Arab, or Eastern cultures have put women in an inferior position no more nor less than have Western culture and Christianity; all the great religions of the world share the same principles regarding the submission of women to men; women's oppression is not due to religion but to a "class and patriarchal system"; women are not mentally inferior to men; Arab women will only be freed by their own efforts; revolutionary change and socialism can accelerate the pace of women's emancipation; Arab women were the first in history to resist the patriarchal system; the traditions and culture of Islam and of the Arabs contain positive aspects for women which must be emphasized while the negative aspects must be rejected; the portrayal of Arab women in Arab literature is not a true image.

This is an arresting book, filled with experiences that women of any culture can identify with even though they may not have shared them.

Shipler, David. *Arab and Jew: Wounded Spirits in a Promised Land.* **New York: Times Books, 1986. 596pp. $22.50. AMEU price: $12.95.**

David Shipler, award-winning correspondent for the *New York Times,* spent five years on assignment in Jerusalem, this "most crucial place of confrontation." In that space of time, he appears to have come to feel with, to appreciate in a deep way, and not simply to report on, the "human dimension of the Arab-Israeli confrontation." His Pulitzer Prize-winning book resulted from his effort to understand how Arabs and Jews see each other, given the ambience of confrontation. "They and their perceptions of each other," Shipler writes, "are the subject here, for the 3.5 million Jews and 2 million Arabs who live in Israel, the West Bank, the Gaza Strip, and the Golan Heights, stand at the point of contact between the military, ethnic, and religious forces of the region."

After a brief introductory historical sketch, the author examines the relationship between Arab and Jew in three "dimensions": aversion — "the engines of war, nationalism, terrorism, and religious absolutism"; images — stereotypes of many kinds; and interaction — cultural and religious affinities and honest efforts at mutual understanding.

Shipler relies upon many and varied resources in his examination of "the attitudes, images, and stereotypes that Arabs and Jews have of one another, the roots of their aversions, and the complex interactions between them in the small territory where they live together under Israeli rule." Among these resources are interviews and firsthand experiences, along with children's literature, school textbooks, newspapers, and films.

Arab and Jew is a colorful and well-written introduction to the complexities of being Jew or Arab in Israel and in the territories under Israeli control today. Shipler offers no answers, no program, no predictions for the future. He tries only to "ask the right questions." In this way he expresses his profound respect for and belief in the spirit of the peoples who inhabit that tortured but promised land.

Smith, Pamela Ann. *Palestine and the Palestinians, 1876-1983.* **New York: St. Martin's Press, 1984. 279pp. $12.95. Glossary, tables, maps, notes, bibliography, index.**

Pamela Ann Smith combines the best of scholars' and journalists' approaches in this complete but concise study of the Palestinian people.

Smith guides the reader from the land of the Palestinians under the Ottomans to the places that became their homes after the diaspora, describing along the way the changes in Palestinian society, the role of Britain, world events, civil war, and Zionist settlement. Finally she examines the formation of the PLO and the factions within it, in the 1930s, the 1950s, and the 1980s.

The author first traveled to the Middle East as a journalist in 1967. This book is based on numerous interviews with Palestinians in the Middle East, the United States, Latin America, and Europe, as well as written materials — some of them archival and unpublished materials not previously available — from London, the United States, France, and from the Institute of Palestine Studies and the PLO's Research Centre in Beirut.

Smith's work is dense but not difficult reading, amply illustrated with maps and charts and carefully documented with notes and bibliography.

Tawil, Raymonda Hawa. *My Home, My Prison.* **London: Zed Books, 1983. 266pp. $7.50. Available in North America from Humanities Press. Postscript.**

Raymonda Tawil, a Palestinian journalist, wrote this gripping account of that period of her life when she suffered under house arrest. From the start, with the author's exchange with an Israeli woman soldier as she waits in the military governor's office, the book deals with questions of women's equality as much as with equality among Israelis, Jordanians, and Palestinians. The military governor announces the fact of her house arrest. "Like all Palestinians," Tawil writes, "I will bear my prison with me in my heart wherever I go. As a woman, I will suffer a double alienation." She vows to "record the story of all my prisons, all my walls. . . ."

Permeating Tawil's life story is the impressive figure of her activist mother, a Palestinian who was born in the United States but who lived her adult life as an Arab patriot in the land of her ancestors. As the mother lived, so lives the daughter, fearlessly struggling in a complicated and violent society.

Tawil knows that throughout her whole life she has been denied her freedom "in many ways: as a Palestinian, belonging to a people deprived of rights and dignity; as a woman in a semifeudal, patriarchal society; as a citizen of a territory under foreign military occupation; as an individual in a traditionalist, oppressive environment that restricts individual liberties." Her story is of isolation, silence, confinement, intimidation, and harassment, but also of solidarity, outspokenness, freedom, fearlessness, and small victories for truth. Reading it is to encounter almost personally these many experiences.

Tlemcani, Rachid. *State and Revolution in Algeria.* **London and Boulder, Colo.: Zed Books and Westview Press, 1986. 220pp. $30. Cloth. List of acronyms, tables, notes, bibliography, index.**

Tlemcani's eight-page bibliography at the back of this book lists not one up-to-date, English-language book on Algeria — let alone one that would be attractive and accessible to the ordinary reader. This striking gap illustrates the lack of attention that has been paid to a country that is unquestionably one of the more significant Third World countries today. To some extent at least, the publication of *State and Revolution in Algeria* fills that gap. It is not a book, however, that will satisfy the newcomer. For the author's primary interest is in the dynamics of the "state" and "revolution" more than it is in introducing his readers to present-day Algeria per se.

In the course of his political analysis of state and revolution, Rachid Tlemcani, a professor at the Institute of Political Science and International Relations in Algiers, examines many of the controversial policies that the government of Algeria has instituted, including a rapid buildup of heavy industry, militant pressure to boost oil prices, and a vigorous foreign policy based on non-alignment. Selected chapter headings give a feel for the direction of Tlemcani's study: The Social Formation of Algeria on the Eve of French Colonialism; Colonial State and Transition to State Power; The Establishment of the Economic State Apparatus and Capital Accumulation; Bureaucratic State Capitalism and Austerity Policy; and Processes of Ideological Mobilization.

Students of political economy will appreciate the author's clear and well-documented treatise on Algeria's experiences with the revolutionary transformation of the state. Readers interested in a popular introduction to this North African country will have to wait for another book — or learn French.

Zabih, Sepehr. *The Mossadegh Era: Roots of the Iranian Revolution.* Chicago: Lake View Press, 1982. 182pp. $6.95. Notes, bibliography, index.

With the overthrow of the Shah in 1979 Iranian researchers like Sepehr Zabih found the freedom they needed to analyze the recent course of events in Iran without fear of reprisal. Studies of the brief reign of the Shah's predecessor, the nationalistic revolutionary leader Dr. Mohammad Mossadegh (1951–53), were, according to Zabih, particularly worrisome to the Shah because Mossadegh's nationalist movement "espoused many liberal-democratic ideas in relation to Iranian political institutions, which strongly appealed to the politically articulate strata of the population. Consequently, the author states, "the regime actively discouraged access to source material on the Mossadegh era and made sure that foreign accounts of this period 'unfavorable to the Shah' would be banned from the country."

Sepehr Zabih knows Iran and this particular period in its history very well. He is the author of numerous highly acclaimed books on Iran and as a journalist and political commentator for *Bakhtare Emrouz* and the London *Times* in the early 1950s he was closely associated with Dr. Mossadegh and his colleagues.

There are a number of reasons why Zabih's historical account of events in Iran more than thirty years ago should interest concerned students of political change today. Chief among them is the fact that the interplay of political forces in the early 1950s—the clerics, the nationalists, the communists, and the Iranian military and its leader, Reza Shah Pahlavi—created the Iran we find today. The clerics, under the leadership of Ayatollah Khomeini, emerged victorious from the 1979 revolution, but as a reading of *The Mossadegh Era* makes clear their position is by no means secure. Another reason for returning to the events of the early 1950s is to understand better the role of the U.S. Central Intelligence Agency—and British intelligence as well—in the overthrow of the Mossadegh government.

Bibliographies

Atiyeh, George N. *The Contemporary Middle East, 1948-1973: A Selective and Annotated Bibliography.* **Boston: G.K. Hall, 1975. 664pp.**
Annotated list of more than six thousand monographs, articles, and pamphlets. Languages include English, French, German, Italian, and Spanish, with a few entries in Arabic, Turkish, and Farsi.

Atiyeh, George N., ed. *Jerusalem Past and Present: An Annotated Bibliography in English.* **New York: Americans for Middle East Understanding, 1975. 32pp.**
A short mimeographed bibliography focused on the city of Jerusalem and containing general works and others about description and travel, planning, history, the significance of Jerusalem, the "Jerusalem question," Jerusalem at the United Nations, and East Jerusalem under Israeli occupation.

Bryson, Thomas A., ed. *United States-Middle East Diplomatic Relations, 1784-1978: An Annotated Bibliography.* **Metuchen, N.J.: Scarecrow Press, 1979. 205pp.**
The preface to this guide offers a survey of bibliographic guides and reference works on U.S. diplomatic involvement in the Middle East. The book itself includes lists of books, articles, documents, and academic dissertations on this subject.

Clements, Frank, ed. *Emergence of Arab Nationalism: From the Nineteenth Century to 1921.* **Wilmington, Del.: Scholarly Resources, 1976.**
Well-annotated catalog of English-language materials on Arab nationalism, excluding North Africa, southern Arabia, and non-Arab Middle Eastern countries.

De Vore, Ronald M., ed. *The Arab-Israeli Conflict: A Historical, Political, Social and Military Bibliography.* **Santa Barbara, Calif.: Clio Books, 1976. Author index.**
Unannotated catalog of published works, well-organized by subject. Absence of a title or subject index weakens this bibliography.

Geddes, C. L. *Guide to Reference Books for Islamic Studies.* **Denver: American Institute of Islamic Studies, 1985. Bibliographic Series, no. 9. 429pp.**
Twelve hundred citations to monographs, articles, maps, and other resources on the history, religion, and culture of the Islamic peoples.

Hussaini, Hatem I., ed. *The Palestine Problem: An Annotated Bibliography, 1967-1974.* **Washington, D.C.: Arab Information Center, 1974. 81pp.**
Annotated guide to published works that either represent the Arab point of view on Palestine or are at least critical of Zionism. Four sections: (1) origins of the Palestinian problem; (2) Israeli occupation and Palestinian resistance; (3) critics of Zionism; and (4) legal and religious aspects of conflict resolution.

Khalidi, Walid, and Jill Khadduri, eds. *Palestine and the Arab-Israeli Conflict: An Annotated Bibliography.* **Beirut: Institute for Palestine Studies, 1974. 736pp. Indexes.**
This substantial work contains annotated references to 4,580 books,

articles, pamphlets, and academic studies published between 1880 and 1971 in a variety of languages. Subjects treated include Zionism, Palestinian history, Arab national politics, and Middle Eastern activities of the United States and Soviet Union.

Le Vine, Victor T., and Timothy Luke. *A Select Bibliography on Arab-American Relations.* **St. Louis, Mo.: Washington University Press, 1977. 23pp.**

A short, mimeographed pamphlet with unannotated lists of books and articles that focus particularly on the politics and economics of oil.

Littlefield, David W., ed. *The Islamic Near East and North Africa: An Annotated Reference Guide to Books in English.* **Littleton, Colo.: Libraries Unlimited, 1977. Indexes.**

This is an excellent introductory bibliography for the serious student as well as for librarians. Littlefield has made a careful selection and his annotations and recommendations for study are very helpful.

Mahler, Gregory S. *Bibliography of Israeli Politics.* **Boulder, Colo., and London: Westview Press, 1985. Westview Special Studies on the Middle East. 133pp. Index.**

A bibliography of English-language monographs, articles, and documents on the political system of the state of Israel. The 1,419 unannotated citations also cover Arab-Israeli relations, the Palestinians, Gaza, and the West Bank.

Schultz, Ann, ed. *International and Regional Politics in the Middle East and North Africa: A Guide to Information Sources.* **Detroit: Gale Research, 1977. 244pp. Indexes.**

The sixth volume in Gale's "International Relations Information Guide" series is divided into subjects relevant to the study of political science. Each section opens with a brief essay.

Sherman, John, ed. *The Arab-Israeli Conflict, 1945-1971: A Bibliography.* **New York: Garland Publishers, 1978. 419pp.**

This bibliography covers the Arab-Israeli conflict from the end of World War II until the death of Egypt's President Nasser in 1970. Sherman's guide is heavily biased in favor of the Israeli point of view.

Simon, Reva S. *The Modern Middle East: A Guide to Research Tools in the Social Sciences.* **Boulder, Colo.: Westview Press, 1978. 283pp.**

Designed for the academic, this guide to reference sources includes works in Middle Eastern and western languages. Annotations are very brief.

Catalogs, Directories, Guides

Grabhorn, Ann, and Robert Staab, eds. *Resource Guide for Middle Eastern Studies.* **Salt Lake City: Middle East Outreach Council, 1984. Rev. ed. 187pp. $15. Second revised edition forthcoming fall 1987. Illustrations, bibliography.**

The 1984 edition of this looseleaf guide is intended for use by Middle East "outreach" personnel at universities, colleges, and other academic institutions. Its wealth of Middle Eastern resources can and should be tapped by educators and activists in other settings as well.

After introductory chapters on the Middle East Outreach Council and the "state of the art" for Middle East outreach, the guide provides descriptive information on national and regional Middle East Outreach programs throughout the United States and a list of U.S. national and regional organizations related to the Middle East. These are followed in turn by sample programs from conferences, seminars, and workshops on Middle Eastern themes.

The final section in the guide is a lengthy "sampler" of films dealing with the Middle East. See audiovisuals chapter below.

Study Guides and Curriculum Materials

Afifi, Ruth, Ayad Al-Qazzaz, and Audrey Shabbas. *The Arab World: A Handbook for Teachers.* **Berkeley, Calif.: Najda, 1978. 128pp. $5.**

An attractive and well-organized guide. Najda and Arab World Consultants should be contacted for updated curriculum materials related to this guide.

Arab World Consultants. *The Arab World: Multi-Media Units.* **Berkeley, Calif.: Arab World Consultants, 1986. Rev. ed.**

These highly regarded curriculum materials are designed to introduce young people (kindergarten through ninth grade) to the Arab world through slides, games, cassettes, posters, and a wealth of activities.

Learning center materials are included, integrating basic skills: reading, writing, math, as well as creative writing, literature, art, and ecological science concepts. Student participation and creativity are encouraged throughout.

The Arab World is designed "to enrich and enhance textbook coverage of an area increasingly important to the world, but long neglected in our schools," state the designers. Each of the six units is self-contained and can be used independently of the others. All materials are produced on heavy-weight cardstock for long wear.

The six units are: (1) *Introduction.* 112 slides and commentary, along with a handbook, atlas, posters, map, student projects, task cards, Saudi-style headdress, a publication in Arabic, and more. (2) *Food, Farming, and Ecology.* Sixty slides showing little-known techniques in land and water use, preservation of ecological systems, use and reuse of environment and resources, and food harvesting, storage, and preservation. Fourteen student projects reinforce concepts while involving participants in food preparation, gardening, and recycling. (3) *Storytelling and Games.* Thirteen slides and some seventeen projects, including: Arab folktales newly translated, retold, and illustrated; dramatic reading, shadow puppetry, theatrical performance; and eight games to construct and play, including field games. (4) *Language, Calligraphy, and Art.* Twenty-five slides, posters on the alphabet and number systems, and more than twenty student projects and activities. Cassette tape with Arabic counting, conversation, songs, and nursery rhymes (with written guide to pronunciation and meaning). (5) *Music and Dance.* Thirteen slides, with seven mini-posters and seven student projects. Cassette tape of music, prayer calls, and Quranic recitation, with second side featuring European/Western music influenced by Arabic music. (6) *Arabs in America.* Twenty-six slides tracing the history of Arabic-speaking Americans from slavery days to mid-nineteenth century waves of immigrants, to present-day Arab-Americans. Learning center materials involve students in the tracing of their own family heritage, as well as oral history and research projects for older students.

Bucher, Henry, Jr. *Middle East.* **Guilford, Conn.: Dushkin Publishing Group, 1984. 160pp. $4.95. Maps, notes, glossary, list of resources, discussion questions, index.**

This volume in Dushkin's "Third World" series departs from standard treatments of the Middle East by focusing attention on five peoples who populate that region: the Copts, Shias, Jews, Armenians, and Palestinians. The author offers three reasons for his choice of these peoples: "(1) their past role in history has been important; (2) they exist today in very different but significant forms; and (3) they represent some major geographical areas, cultures, and religions – often cutting across present national boundaries."

A further stated aim of this guide is "to introduce the student to the immense complexity of the Middle East and to provide interpretative perspectives and bibliographical tools for further study."

The final chapter discusses "modern Zionism and Palestinian nationalism."

In Search of Reconciliation: A Study Guide. **New York: Middle East Office of the United Church of Christ and the Christian Church (Disciples of Christ), 1986. $30.**

The format of this study guide is a seven-session program for a group of eight to twelve persons. The seven hour-long sessions cover: introductory material, Judaism, Islam, Christianity, Palestinian and Jewish homelands, Lebanon and Iran/Iraq wars, and U.S. involvement and world peace.

Materials included in the guide are two videotapes, one set of background articles for reproduction, a facilitator's guide, an annotated bibliography, and suggestions for how local congregations can act on Middle East issues.

In Search of Reconciliation addresses many questions that would be on the minds of concerned church people and others, such as: What are the causes of terrorism? What is Zionism? Who and what is the Palestine Liberation Organization? What is the role of the Christian church as a minority in the Middle East? What are U.S. interests in the region? Should local congregations participate in advocacy regarding the Middle East? If so, how?

In Whose Interest: A Middle East Discussion Packet. **New York: Mobilization for Survival, 1985. $5.**

In Whose Interest is a packet of five group-study units – each including one background reading and a set of discussion questions. The material, designed for peace and anti-nuclear groups, explores U.S. foreign policy in the Middle East, focusing primarily on the basics of Middle East politics and the role the U.S. government plays in that region.

The packet does a particular service: it speaks to the fear most people have of discussing the Middle East because they fear the subject is too complex or emotionally charged. The packet presents various views of the U.S. peace movement and is intended to help activists find a common ground of understanding and collaboration.

Nijim, Basheer K. *The Arab World: Exercises in Population Characteristics.* **Cedar Falls: University of Northern Iowa, Geography Dept., June 1983. 26pp.**

This booklet contains five self-contained exercises, or units, dealing with various population and geographic dimensions of the Arab World (excluding the Palestine Liberation Organization). Each unit specifies its objectives, the materials needed, procedure to be followed in preparing maps and graphs, and questions for interpreting the results obtained. Maps and graph paper are supplied.

Pearson, Robert P. *Through Middle Eastern Eyes.* **New York: Center for International Training and Education, 1984. Rev. ed. 254pp. $15.95.**

Through Middle Eastern Eyes begins from an admirable perspective: it "does not try to *explain* the Middle East, but endeavors to *show* it." Its double objective is "to let Middle Easterners speak for themselves, and to let readers think for themselves."

In the ten years that followed the publication of the first edition of this book in 1975 Egypt and Israel signed the Camp David Accords, the Shah of Iran was overthrown, Lebanon was invaded by the Israeli military, and Iran and Iraq engaged in war. All of these issues are touched upon in this new edition, but—notes the editor of this series—"other aspects of the Middle East, such as the history of the region, the tenets of Islam, and the cultural practices of the people, are far more enduring and have changed very little, if at all, in the past decade."

A skillful blend of the eternal and the transient, this book "attempts to recreate the reality of everyday life as experienced by Middle Easterners themselves." Designed especially for high school students, this text makes use of firsthand accounts by Middle Easterners, autobiographies, and fiction. The text has a companion volume with teaching ideas and lesson plans.

Presbyterian Church (U.S.A.). *A Middle East Study/Action Packet.* **Atlanta: Presbyterian Church (U.S.A.), 1985. $9.75. Bibliography.**

This packet was developed for use during a two-year study program on the Middle East conducted throughout the Presbyterian Church in the United States. It contains a study guide that outlines an eight-week course for church groups, along with additional suggestions for ways to introduce Middle East issues in shorter periods of time.

Also included are church policy statements, a paper on the Christian presence in the Middle East, several publications about Zionism and the

U.S. link to Israel, a United Nations pamphlet on the status of Palestinians, an issue paper on Iranian refugees as a persecuted group, a booklet on Christian-Muslim relations, and more.

Reese, Lyn, and Jean Wilkenson, eds. *Women in the World: Annotated History Resources for the Secondary Student.* **Metuchen, N.J.: Scarecrow Press, forthcoming 1987.**

This well-designed and fully annotated guide to educational materials for the secondary school student contains print and nonprint resources on women in North Africa and the Middle East. Highly recommended.

Reference Books

Laqueur, Walter, and Barry Rubin, eds. *The Israel-Arab Reader: A Documentary History of the Middle East Conflict.* **New York: Viking Penguin, 1985. Rev. ed. 704pp. $7.95. Map, documentation, bibliography.**

This handy reference book offers a unique and contemporary collection of speeches, letters, treaties, reports, and other documents on the full spectrum of the Israeli-Arab conflict, from the earliest Zionist manifestoes to the Camp David Accords and the May 1983 Lebanon-Israel truce agreement. The materials are arranged chronologically and a wide range of viewpoints are represented.

Legum, Colin, Haim Shaked, and Daniel Dishon, eds. *Middle East Contemporary Survey. Vol. VI: 1981-82.* **New York: Holmes & Meier, 1984. 957pp. $170. Volumes I through V are available at $170 each.**

The sixth volume in this series contains essays by some three dozen contributors on political conditions in the Middle East in 1982. The contributors are drawn largely from the Dayan Center for Middle Eastern and African Studies of Tel Aviv University. Also included are specialists from universities in the United States, Britain, France, Germany, and the Middle East.

Lenczowski, George. *The Middle East in World Affairs.* **Ithaca, N.Y.: Cornell University Press, 1980. 4th ed. 862pp. Map, index, bibliography, appendix.**

This text sets itself a lofty goal: "to give a comprehensive account of the political developments in the Middle East since 1914, including those in international relations, regional affairs, and domestic politics in individual countries." George Lenczowski, professor of political science at the University of California, Berkeley, opens this book with a series of historical essays and then proceeds on a country-by-country basis to articles on Turkey, Iran, Afghanistan, Iraq, Syria, Lebanon, Israel, Jordan, Egypt, Saudi Arabia, Yemen, South Yemen, and the Persian Gulf. The North African Arab Maghreb (Morocco, Tunisia, Algeria, and Libya) are not discussed, except as they have participated in the broader Arab unity efforts.

The Middle East and North Africa 1987. **London: Europa Publications, 1986. 33rd ed. 911pp. Statistical tables, bibliography, maps.**

This reference work is divided into three parts: (1) General Survey (pp.3–196), (2) Regional Organizations (pp. 197–254), and (3) Country Surveys (pp. 255–911). The country surveys cover twenty-four nations, from Afghanistan in the east to Morocco in the west. Bibliographies of books and serial publications and organizational directories are provided throughout the book.

Middle East Economic Handbook. **London: Euromonitor, 1986. 487pp. $80. Cloth. Statistical tables, charts, maps.**

This is a convenient source of data on the economies of sixteen nations of the Middle East and North Africa. The handbook opens with an economic overview of the region, its role in the world economy, and its prospects for the future. The bulk of the guide consists of lengthy profiles of each of the sixteen countries. Profiles contain discussions and statistics on the country's economy, including national income, political system, population and labor force, industry, energy, agriculture, health, education, transport and communication, foreign trade and balance of payments, and tourism.

The handbook includes nearly 375 tables and charts.

O'Brien, Lee. *American Jewish Organizations and Israel*. **Washington, D.C.: Institute of Palestine Studies, June 1986. 238pp. $24.95. AMEU price: $13.95. Appendix, bibliography, index.**

This is a meticulously researched guide to the organizational structure, funding, program activities, and political role of American Jewish pro-Israel groups, both Zionist organizations and community organizations. O'Brien describes the pro-Israel lobby and details their target areas (e.g., campuses and churches). He also covers "special focus organizations" such as the Youth Institute for Peace in the Middle East, Americans for a Safe Israel, and the National Committee for Labor Israel.

Partington, David H., ed. *The Middle East Annual: Issues and Events. Vol.5 – 1985*. **Boston: G. K. Hall, 1986. 210pp. $49.95. Cloth. Maps, chronology, bibliography, index.**

The fifth volume in this highly acclaimed series opens with a forty-three-page chronicle of political events, or happenings of political import, in the Middle East in 1985. All citations in this chronicle are taken from the *New York Times*.

Four substantive essays and two updates (on the Iran-Iraq war and on Afghanistan) occupy the next 110 pages of *The Middle East Annual*. The articles concern women in Islamic law and ideology, political changes in Sudan, Pakistan under Zia ul-Haq, and the "Cyprus problem."

The third and final part of the book offers a bibliography of monographs and serials in English, French, and German that appeared in 1985. Entries are restricted to those works that deal with the modern Middle East, with historical works included only when they provide the background necessary to understand contemporary events. About one-half of the entries are annotated, from secondary sources in some cases.

Earlier volumes in this series are still available.

SUPPLEMENTARY LIST OF BOOKS

MIDDLE EAST GENERAL

Abdel-Kalek, Anouar, ed. *Contemporary Arab Political Thought.* Trans. Michael Pallis. London: Zed Books, 1983. 254pp. $11.50.

Allan, J. A., ed. *Libya since Independence: Economic and Social Development.* New York: St. Martin's Press, 1982. 210pp. $22.50. Cloth.

Amin, Samir. *The Arab Nation: Nationalism and Class Struggles.* London: Zed Books, 1976. 116pp. $7.95.

Bushnaq, Inea. *Arab Folktales.* New York: Pantheon Books, 1986. 386pp. $19.95. AMEU price: $10.95.

Chacour, Elias. *Blood Brothers.* Grand Rapids, Mich.: Chosen Books, 1984. 224pp. $6.95. AMEU price: $4.95.

Chafets, Ze'ev. *Double Vision: How the American Press Distorts Our View of the Middle East.* New York: Morrow, 1984. 383pp. $16.95.

Critchfield, Richard. *Shahhat: An Egyptian.* Syracuse, N.Y.: Syracuse University Press, 1978. 264pp. $9.95.

Faris, Hani A. *Arab Nationalism and the Future of the Arab World.* Belmont, Mass.: Association of Arab-American University Graduates, 1987. 170pp. $13. Monograph 22.

Freedman, Robert O., ed. *The Middle East: After the Israeli Invasion of Lebanon.* Syracuse, N.Y.: Syracuse University Press, 1986. 364pp. $14.95.

Ghareeb, Edmund, ed. *Split Vision: The Portrayal of Arabs in the American Media.* Washington, D.C.: American-Arab Affairs Council, 1983. 171pp. $6.95.

Halsell, Grace. *Prophecy and Politics: Militant Evangelists on a Path to Nuclear War.* Westport, Conn.: Lawrence Hill & Co., 1986. 210pp. $14.95. AMEU price: $8.95.

Hetata, Sherif. *The Net.* London: Zed Books, 1986. 220pp. $7.95.

Hiro, Dilip. *Inside the Middle East.* New York: McGraw-Hill, 1982. $8.95.

Nijim, Basheer. *American Church Politics and the Middle East.* Belmont, Mass.: Association of Arab-American University Graduates, 1982. 156pp. $6.95.

Perry, Glenn E. *A Resource Guide to Materials on the Arab World.* Belmont, Mass.: Association of Arab-American University Graduates, 1986. 145pp. $10. Monograph 21.

Polk, William R. *The Arab World.* Cambridge, Mass.: Harvard University Press, 1980. 4th ed. 456pp.

Rugh, Andrea B. *Family in Contemporary Egypt.* Syracuse, N.Y.: Syracuse University Press, 1984. 320pp. $14.95.

Schenker, Hillel, ed. *After Lebanon: The Israeli-Palestinian Connection.* New York: Pilgrim Press, 1985. 320pp. $18.95. Cloth.

Shaheen, Jack G. *The TV Arab.* Bowling Green, Ohio: Bowling Green State University Popular Press, 1984. 146pp. $6.95. AMEU price: $4.95.

El-Shazly, Saad. *The Arab Military Option.* San Francisco: American Mideast Research, 1986. 329pp. $26. AMEU price: $15.50.

Woolfson, Marion. *Prophets in Babylon: Jews in the Arab World.* London: Faber & Faber, 1980. 292pp. $32.95. Cloth.

Foreign Relations

Cleveland, Ray. *The Middle East and South Asia.* Washington, D.C.: Stryker-Post Publications, 1986. 132pp. $5.50. AMEU price: $4.25.

Dann, Uriel, ed. *The Great Powers in the Middle East: 1919-1939. Regional Policies in Their Global Context.* New York: Holmes & Meier, 1985. 320pp. $39.50. Cloth.

Hallaba, Saadallah A. S. *Euro-Arab Dialogue.* Brattleboro, Vt.: Amana Books, 1985. $6.95.

Ismael, Tareq Y. *International Relations of the Contemporary Middle East: A Study in World Politics.* Syracuse, N.Y.: Syracuse University Press, 1986. 290pp. $14.95.

Neff, Donald. *Warriors at Suez: Eisenhower Takes America into the Middle East.* New York: Linden Press/Simon & Schuster, 1981. 480pp. $17.95.

Tillman, Seth P. *The United States in the Middle East.* Bloomington, Ind.: Indiana University Press, 1984. 352pp. $9.95.

Islam

Dekmejian, R. Hrair. *Islam in Revolution: Fundamentalism in the Arab World.* Syracuse, N.Y.: Syracuse University Press, 1985. 250pp. $13.95.

Esposito, John L. *Islam and Politics.* Syracuse: Syracuse University Press, 1984. 288pp. $12.95.

Haddad, Y., B. Haines, and E. Findly, eds. *The Islamic Impact.* Syracuse, N.Y.: Syracuse University Press, 1984. 264pp. $13.95. AMEU price: $8.

MacEoin, Denis, and Ahmed Al-Shahi, eds. *Islam in the Modern World*. New York: St. Martin's Press, 1983. 240pp. $22.50. Cloth.

Mortimer, Edward. *Faith and Power: The Politics of Islam*. New York: Random House, 1982. 432pp. $9.95. AMEU price: $7.75.

Stowasser, Barbara Freyer, ed. *The Islamic Impulse*. London and Sydney: Croom Helm, in cooperation with the Center for Contemporary Arab Studies, Georgetown University (Washington, D.C.), 1987. 330pp.

Wright, Robin. *Sacred Rage: The Crusade of Militant Islam*. New York: Simon and Schuster/Touchstone, 1986. 336pp. $7.95. AMEU price: $5.75.

Arab-Israeli Relations

Curtiss, Richard. *A Changing Image: American Perceptions of the Arab-Israeli Dispute*. Washington, D.C.: American Educational Trust, 1982. 216pp. $14.95. AMEU price: $8.95.

Hirst, David. *The Gun and the Olive Branch*. London: Futura Publications, 1978. 367pp. $7.95. First edition reprinted in 1983. AMEU price: $2.75.

Khouri, Fred J. *The Arab-Israeli Dilemma*. Syracuse, N.Y.: Syracuse University Press, 1985. 605pp. $12.95. AMEU price: $7.95.

Mroz, John Edwin. *Beyond Security: Private Perceptions among Arabs and Israelis*. Elmsford, N.Y.: Pergamon Press, 1981. 202pp. $8.95.

Oil

Luciani, Giacomo. *The Oil Companies and the Arab World*. New York: St. Martin's Press, 1984. 208pp. $25. Cloth.

Peterson, J. E., ed. *The Politics of Middle Eastern Oil*. Washington, D.C.: Middle East Institute, 1984. 530pp. $14.95.

Terzian, Pierre. *OPEC: The Inside Story*. Trans. Michael Pallis. London: Zed Books, 1985. 355pp. $12.25.

Women

Fernea, Elizabeth Warnock. *A Street in Marrakech: A Personal Encounter with the Lives of Moroccan Women*. Garden City, N.Y.: Anchor Press/Doubleday, 1976. 419pp. $3.50.

Fernea, Elizabeth Warnock, ed. *Women and the Family in the Middle East: New Voices of Change*. Austin: University of Texas Press, 1985. 356pp.

Hussain, Freeda. *Muslim Women*. New York: St. Martin's Press, 1984. 240pp. $22.50.

Mernissi, Fatima. *Beyond the Veil: Male-Female Dynamics in a Modern Muslim Society*. New York and London: Schenkman Publishing Co., 1975. 132pp. $5.95.

Minai, Maila. *Women in Islam: Tradition and Transition in the Middle East*. New York: Seaview Books, 1981. 284pp. $12.95. Cloth.

Phizacklea, Annie, ed. *One Way Ticket: Migration and Female Labour*. London and Boston: Routledge and Kegan Paul, 1983. 162pp. $8.95.

Walther, Wiebke. *Woman in Islam.* Totowa, N.J.: Rowman and Allanheld, 1982. 204pp. $35. Cloth.

ARABIAN PENINSULA AND GULF

Aliboni, Roberto. *The Red Sea Region.* Syracuse, N.Y.: Syracuse University Press, 1985. 144pp. Cloth.

Azari, Farah, ed. *Women of Iran.* London: Ithaca Press, 1984. $8.00.

Bulloch, John. *The Persian Gulf Unveiled.* London: Congdon & Weed, 1985. 240pp. $16.95. Distributed in North America by St. Martin's Press.

Al-Ebraheem, Hassan Ali. *Kuwait and the Gulf: Small States and the International System.* New York: St. Martin's Press, 1983. 200pp. $25. Cloth.

Eickelman, Christine. *Women and Community in Oman.* New York: New York University Press, 1985. 240pp. $10.

Field, Michael. *The Merchants: The Big Business Families of Saudi Arabia and All the Gulf States.* New York: Viking, 1985. 384pp. $18.95.

Ismael, Jacqueline S. *Kuwait: Social Change in Historical Perspective.* Syracuse, N.Y.: Syracuse University Press, 1982. 224pp. $22. Cloth.

Meo, Leila, ed. *U.S. Strategy in the Gulf: Intervention against Liberation.* Belmont, Mass.: Association of Arab-American University Graduates, 1981. 130pp. $6. Monograph 14.

Niblock, Tim, ed. *State, Society and Economy in Saudi Arabia.* New York: St. Martin's Press, 1981. 314pp. $29.95. Cloth.

Young, Arthur N. *Saudi Arabia: The Making of a Financial Giant.* New York: New York University Press, 1983. 162pp. Cloth.

FERTILE CRESCENT

Israel and the Jews

El-Asmar, Fouzi. *Through the Hebrew Looking Glass.* London: Zed Press, 1985. 176pp. $9.25. AMEU price: $5.95.

Aishai, Bernard. *The Tragedy of Zionism.* New York: Farrar, Strauss, Giroux, 1985. 384pp. $18.95.

Avnery, Uri. *My Friend, The Enemy.* London: Zed Press, 1985. 352pp. $9.95.

Bahbah, Bishara. *Israel and Latin America: The Military Connection.* New York: St. Martin's Press, 1986. 210pp. $12.95. AMEU price: $7.50.

Feuerlicht, Roberta Strauss. *The Fate of the Jews: A People Torn between Israeli Power and Jewish Ethics.* New York: Times Books, 1983. 324pp. $18.95.

Halsell, Grace. *Journey to Jerusalem.* New York: Macmillan Publishers, 1982. 193pp. $7.95. AMEU price: $3.50.

Harkabi, Yehoshafar. *The Bar Kokhba Syndrome: Risk and Realism in

International Politics. Chappaqua, N.Y.: Rossel Books, 1983. 206pp. $15.95. AMEU price: $12.50.

Hertzberg, Arthur, ed. *Zionist Idea: A Historical Analysis and Reader.* New York: Atheneum, 1969. $7.95.

Hunter, Jane. *Israeli Foreign Policy: South Africa and Central America.* Boston: South End Press, 1987. 274pp. $9.50.

Lilienthal, Alfred. *The Zionist Connection.* New Brunswick, N.J: North American, 1982. 904pp. $9.95. AMEU price: $6.50.

Lustick, Ian. *Arabs in the Jewish State: Israel's Control of a National Minority.* Austin: University of Texas Press, 1981. 400pp. $10.95.

Nakhleh, Khalil, and Clifford A. Wright. *After the Palestine-Israel War: Limits to U.S. and Israeli Policy.* Belmont, Mass.: Institute of Arab Studies, 1983. 130pp. $7.95.

Neff, Donald. *Warriors for Jerusalem: Six Days That Changed the Middle East.* New York: Simon and Schuster, 1984. 384pp. $17.95.

Rein, Natalie. *Daughters of Rachel: Women in Israel.* New York: Penguin Books, 1980. 182pp. $4.95.

Saba, Michael. *The Armageddon Network.* Brattleboro, Vt.: Amana Books, 1984. 288pp. $9.95. AMEU price: $5.95.

Segev, Tom. *1949: The First Israelis.* New York: Macmillan/Free Press, 1986. 379pp. $19.95. AMEU price: $11.95.

Sharif, Regina. *Non-Jewish Zionism.* London: Zed Books, 1983. 144pp. $8.75. AMEU price: $5.50.

Tivnan, Edward. *The Lobby: Jewish Political Power and American Foreign Policy.* New York: Simon and Schuster, 1987. 304pp. $19.95. Cloth.

Jordan

Cordesman, Anthony H. *Jordanian Arms and the Middle East Balance.* Washington, D.C.: Middle East Institute, 1984. 186pp. $15.

Gubser, Peter. *Jordan: Crossroads of Middle Eastern Events.* Boulder, Colo.: Westview Press, 1983. 139pp. $12.95.

Lebanon

Ajami, Fouad. *The Vanished Imam: Musa al Sadr and the Shia of Lebanon.* Ithaca, N.Y.: Cornell University Press, 1986. 228pp. $17.95. AMEU price: $9.95.

Ball, George W. *Error and Betrayal in Lebanon.* Washington, D.C.: Foundation for Middle East Peace, 1984. 158pp. $7.95.

Gabriel, Richard A. *Operation Peace for Galilee: The Israeli-PLO War in Lebanon.* New York: Hill and Wang, 1985. 256pp. $7.95.

Gilmour, David. *Lebanon: The Fractured Country.* New York: St. Martin's Press, 1983. 225pp. $8.95. AMEU price: $6.50.

Nassib, Selim, and Caroline Tisdall. *Beirut: Frontline Story.* Trenton, N.J.: Africa World Press, 1983. 160pp. $6.95.

Odeh, B. J. *Lebanon: Dynamics of Conflict.* London: Zed Press, 1985. 256pp. $9.95.

Petran, Tabitha. *The Struggle over Lebanon.* New York: Monthly Review Press, 1984. 320pp. $12.

Schiff, Ze'ev, and Ehud Ya'ari. *Israel's Lebanon War.* Trans. Ina Friedman. New York: Simon and Schuster, 1984. $17.95.

Yermiya, Dov. *My War Diary: Lebanon, June 5 - July 1, 1982.* Boston: South End Press, 1984. 120pp. $7.

Palestine and the Palestinians

Aruri, Naseer, ed. *Occupation: Israel over Palestine.* Belmont, Mass. Association of Arab-American University Graduates, 1983. 467pp. $13.50. AMEU price: $8.50.

Becker, Jillian. *The PLO: The Rise and Fall of the Palestine Liberation Organization.* New York: St. Martin's Press, 1984. 288pp. $19.95.

Chapman, Colin. *Whose Promised Land?* Herts, England: Lion Publishing, 1983. 253pp. $3.95.

Dimbleby, Jonathan. *The Palestinians.* London and New York: Quartet Books, 1979. 256pp. £12.50. Cloth. Photographs by Donald McCullin.

Diqs, Isaak. *A Bedouin Boyhood.* New York: Universe Books, 1983. 176pp. $10.40. AMEU price: $7.

Ekin, Larry. *Enduring Witness: The Churches and the Palestinians.* Geneva: Oikoumene, 1985. 135pp. $6.25. AMEU price: $4.95.

Frangi, Abdallah. *The PLO and Palestine.* London: Zed Books, 1982. 256pp. $9.95.

Graham-Brown, Sarah. *Palestinians and Their Society: 1880-1946.* London: Quartet Books, 1980. 184pp. $14.95. AMEU price: $7.50.

Gresh, Alain. *The PLO: The Struggle Within.* London: Zed Press, 1985. 288pp. $9.95.

Hallan Bin Talal. *Palestinian Self-Determination: A Study of the West Bank and Gaza Strip.* New York: Quartet Books, 1981. 138pp. $14.95.

Hart, Alan. *Arafat: Terrorist or Peacemaker?* London: Sidgwick and Jackson, 1985. 501pp. $21.95. AMEU price: $12.95.

Khalidi, Rashid. *Under Siege: P.L.O. Decision-making During the 1982 War.* New York: Columbia University Press, 1986. 241pp. $25. AMEU price: $13.95.

Abu-Lughod, Ibrahim, ed. *Palestinian Rights: Affirmation and Denial.* Wilmette, Ill.: Medina Press, 1982. 225pp. $8.

Mallison, W. Thomas, and Sally V. Mallison. *The Palestine Problem in International Law and World Order.* Harlow, England: Longman Ltd., 1986. 564pp. $39.95. AMEU price: $24.50.

Rosenbluth, Marty. *Migrants to Their Own Land.* Belmont, Mass.: Association of Arab-American University Graduates, 1987. Forthcoming.

Saraste, Leena. *For Palestine.* London: Zed Press, 1985. 96pp. $12.25.

Shadid, Mohammed Khalil. *The United States and the Palestinians.* New York: St. Martin's Press, 1981. 252pp. $26.

Occupied Territories

Lesch, Ann Mosely. *Political Perceptions of the Palestinians on the West Bank and the Gaza Strip.* Washington, D.C.: Middle East Institute, 1980. 114pp. $5.50.

Metzger, Jan, M. Orth, and C. Sterzing. *This Land Is Our Land: The West Bank under Israeli Occupation.* London: Zed Press, 1980. 288pp. $10.25.

Richardson, John P. *The West Bank: A Portrait.* Washington, D.C.: Middle East Institute, 1984. 221pp. $9.95.

Abu Shakrah, J., et al. *Israeli Settler Violence in the Occupied Territories: 1980-1984.* Chicago: Palestine Human Rights Campaign, 1985. 125pp. $7.95. AMEU price: $5.95.

Shinar, Dov. *Palestinian Voices: Communication and Nation Building in the West Bank.* Boulder, Colo.: Lynne Rienner, 1987. 212pp. $25. Cloth.

Thorpe, Merle. *Prescription for Conflict: Israel's West Bank Settlement Policies.* Washington, D.C.: Foundation for Middle East Peace, 1984. 182pp. $7.95.

IRAN

Albert, David H., ed. *Tell the American People: Perspectives on the Iranian Revolution.* Philadelphia: Movement for a New Society, 1980. 176pp. $3.80.

El Azhary, M. S. *The Iran-Iraq War: Historical, Economic and Political Analysis.* New York: St. Martin's Press, 1984. 160pp. $22.50. Cloth.

Bakhash, Shaul. *The Reign of the Ayatollahs: Iran and the Islamic Revolution.* New York: Basic Books, 1986. 292pp. $9.95.

Banuazizi, Ali, and Myron Weiner, eds. *The State, Religion, and Ethnic Politics: Afghanistan, Iran, and Pakistan.* Syracuse, N.Y.: Syracuse University Press, 1986. 390pp. $35. Cloth.

Bashiriyeh, Hossein. *The State and Revolution in Iran: 1962-1982.* New York: St. Martin's Press, 1984. 256pp. $27.50. Cloth.

Bayat, Assef. *Workers and Revolution in Iran: A Third World Experience of Workers' Control.* London: Zed Press, 1985. 304pp. $9.95.

Keddie, Nikki R., and Eric Hooglund, eds. *The Iranian Revolution and the Islamic Republic.* Syracuse, N.Y.: Syracuse University Press, 1986. 264pp. $14.95.

Ladjevardi, Habib. *Labor Unions and Autocracy in Iran.* Syracuse, N.Y.: Syracuse University Press, 1985. 328pp. $29.95. Cloth.

Legum, Colin, ed. *Iran: The Revolution and Beyond.* New York: Holmes & Meier, 1985. 190pp. $14.50.

Mottahedeh, Roy. *The Mantle of the Prophet: Religion and Politics in Iran.* New York: Pantheon Books, 1985. 416pp. $9.95. AMEU price: $6.95.

Stempel, John D. *Inside the Iranian Revolution.* Bloomington, Ind.: Indiana University Press, 1981. 336pp. Cloth.

Taheri, Amir. *The Spirit of Allah: Khomeini and the Islamic Revolution.* New York: Adler & Adler, 1986. 350pp. $18.95. Cloth.

Zabih, Sepehr. *Iran since the Revolution.* Baltimore: Johns Hopkins University Press, 1982. 247pp. $21.50.

IRAQ

Ghareeb, Edmund. *The Kurdish Question in Iraq.* Syracuse, N.Y.: Syracuse University Press, 1981. 240pp. $12.95.

Helms, Christine Moss. *Iraq: Eastern Flank of the Arab World.* Washington, D.C.: Brookings Institution, 1984. 215pp. $9.95.

Niblock Tim. *Iraq: The Contemporary State.* New York: St. Martin's Press, 1982. 283pp. $27.50.

INFORMATION SOURCES

For lists of other books on the Middle East see the bibliographies, catalogs, and reference books described in this chapter above, as well as the major academic journals (e.g., *The Middle East Journal*) described in the periodicals chapter below. See also the quarterly newsletter *Arab Book World* published by Joseph Atallah, 12021 Nieta Dr., Garden Grove, CA 92640 ($48/yr. 28 cm. 16pp.).

To keep current on new releases we suggest that you request book catalogs from the publishers represented in this chapter. Americans for Middle East Understanding and the publishers of *Washington Report on Middle East Affairs* (see periodicals chapter below) both publish excellent catalogs of discounted books on the Middle East.

See also the publications from **Third World Resources,** described in the preface to this resource directory.

3

Periodicals

This chapter is divided into three parts: annotated entries, supplementary list of periodicals, and sources of additional information on periodicals related to the Middle East.

Information in the **annotated entries** is given in the following order: title; publisher; address; frequency of publication; format (magazine, newsletter, newspaper); size (height in centimeters and number of pages); subscription costs; keyword description of format; and description of content.

Quotation marks in the annotations enclose the words of the periodical's publisher or editor, or are taken from promotional materials about the periodical.

Periodicals in the **supplementary list** (pp.64–66) are listed alphabetically and include title; address; frequency of publication; and type of periodical.

The **information sources** part (p. 67) provides information about directories and guides that contain the names of other periodicals related to the Middle East.

All periodical titles and related organizations in this chapter are listed in the appropriate indexes at the back of the directory. Check through the annotated entries part of the organizations chapter, above, for the names of additional periodicals.

ANNOTATED ENTRIES

Ahfad Journal: Women and Change, **Ahfad University for Women, P.O. Box 167, Omdurman, Sudan. 2 issues/yr. Magazine. 24 cm. 94pp. Individual subscription: $20/yr. Institutional subscription: $35/yr. Research notes, advertisements, book reviews, editorials, feature articles, network news, comment and analysis, statistical tables.**
This interdisciplinary journal was launched in 1983 to reflect the

"growing importance of research" at Ahfad University for Women. *Ahfad Journal* publishes "original contributions consisting of reports of research, historical or critical analyses, literature reviews, comments, and book reviews, pertaining to the status of women in developing countries and the role of women in development, as well as contributions to the family sciences, psychology and the social sciences, preschool education, and organizational management."

This journal is noteworthy for the unique perspective it brings to critical issues for women in developing countries.

AJME News, **Americans for Justice in the Middle East, P.O. Box 113-5581, Beirut, Lebanon. 12 issues/yr. Newsletter. 28 cm. 12pp. Free with membership of $15/yr. Reports, book reviews, feature articles, network news, poetry, illustrations, photographs, chronology, annual index.**

Coverage of the news in *AJME News* strongly favors Lebanon. Articles on this topic cover civil strife and the family, living with the reality of kidnapping, a Shiite cleric's views on the Lebanese crisis, the Israeli invasion, "breadline inflation" in Lebanon, the situation of Palestinians in Lebanon, and U.S. relations with Lebanon.

Articles on areas other than Lebanon have analyzed the Camp David Accords, critically examined the "Exodus myth," described the stamps and postal history of Palestine, offered an Arab point of view on terrorism, and assessed the Reagan Administration's Middle East policy.

This newsletter celebrated its twelfth year of publication in 1987. All of vol. 11 was devoted to a chronology of the Middle East conflict.

Al Awdah, **Palestine Press Services, P.O. Box 19563, East Jerusalem, Via Israel. 52 issues/yr. Magazine. 28 cm. 32pp. Individual and institutional subscriptions: $100/yr. in North America. Apply for other rates. Feature articles, book reviews, editorials, documentation, news reports, comment and analysis, photographs, chronology.**

This magazine is subtitled: "the only English language Palestinian weekly magazine in the Israeli-occupied territories." Frequently harassed by Israeli military authorities the courageous editors of *Al Awdah* call attention to the fact that their reports on Palestinian affairs (including the activities of the Palestine Liberation Organization) are considered to be "illegal reading material in the Occupied West Bank and Gaza Strip." *Al Awdah* demands the right "to distribute throughout all of the Occupied Land," the editors write, "and calls on all Palestinian national institutions, Israeli democratic forces, and international bodies to support this basic and legitimate demand."

Regular features of the weekly magazine include a chronology of "life under occupation" and a weekly record of Palestinians sentenced by Israeli military courts. Articles cover human rights abuses, corporate news as it affects Palestinians in Israel and elsewhere, Islamic affairs, and more.

American Arab Affairs, **American-Arab Affairs Council, 1730 M St., Suite 411, Washington, DC 20036. 4 issues/yr. Magazine. 25 cm. 180pp.**

Individual and institutional subscriptions: $20/yr. Single issue: $5. Feature articles, advertisements, book reviews, documentation, interviews, statistical tables, notes, bibliography.

The aim of this quarterly journal is "to provide a forum for viewpoints on recent developments that affect U.S.-Arab relations." These "recent developments" range from world oil prices to the sale of U.S. weapons to Saudi Arabia and from non-violent struggle in the West Bank to the activities of the Gulf Cooperation Council.

Book reviews are lengthy. The documentation section regularly numbers twenty pages.

Arab Studies Quarterly, **Association of Arab-American University Graduates, 556 Trapelo Rd., Belmont, MA 02178. 4 issues/yr. Magazine. 22 cm. 130pp. Individual subscription: $16/yr. Institutional subscription: $35/yr. Single issue: $5. Feature articles, advertisements, book reviews, book notices, statistical tables, notes, references.**

This journal, a joint publication of the Association of Arab-American University Graduates and the Institute for Arab Studies, began its ninth year of publication in 1987. The quarterly presents "critical works on Arab society, polity, economy, and history with the aim of combatting entrenched misconceptions and distortions about an important area in today's world."

In addition to regular articles on "the Arabs, their culture, history, and institutions," *Arab Studies Quarterly* also occasionally devotes an entire issue to themes such as: modern Arab writers; the politics of the Middle East; the impact of money in the Middle East; and the dynamics of power and dependency in the Arab world.

Education under Occupation, **North American Academics in Solidarity with Palestine Universities (NAASPU), 220 S. State St., Suite 1308, Chicago, IL 60604. 4 issues/yr. Newsletter. 28 cm. 8pp. Donation requested. News reports, documentation, photographs.**

In the summer of 1985 the Chicago-based Palestine Human Rights Campaign sponsored a trip for a group of U.S. professors to study the issue of academic freedom in the territories occupied by Israel. Together with PHRC these U.S. academics established NAASPU in order to develop "a North American network of academics to acquaint the academic community with the apartheid policies that Palestinian academics and students suffer under Israeli occupation."

This newsletter was launched in early 1986 to further the educational and support activities of the NAASPU. The editors state that they are especially concerned about this issue because "it is our [U.S.] tax monies which provide the Israeli Military the resources to maintain repression."

Al-Fajr Jerusalem, **2025 I St., NW, Suite 902, Washington, DC 20006. 52 issues/yr. Newspaper. 38.5 cm. 16pp. Individual and institutional subscriptions: $40/yr. Student rate: $25/yr. Inquire for rates outside of North America.**

"Much of what Palestinians are saying and doing in the occupied territories is ignored by the international and American press," the editors of this newspaper charge. Since April 1980 *Al-Fajr* has tried to remedy this situation by documenting human rights violations of the Israeli occupation forces, fostering the cultural heritage of the Palestinians with reports on art, literature, and festivals, and offering a Palestinian perspective on U.S. and European policies in the Middle East and the diplomatic activities of the Palestine Liberation Organization.

Al-Haq Newsletter, **Al-Haq/Law in the Service of Man, P.O. Box 1413, Ramallah, West Bank, Via Israel. 6 issues/yr. Newsletter. 29 cm. 12pp. Free with membership in al-Haq. Apply for rates. News reports, documentation.**

The West Bank affiliate of the International Commission of Jurists publishes its bimonthly newsletter (in Arabic, French, and English-language versions) in order to describe al-Haq's legal and human rights work and to report on developments in the West Bank. The editors state that they have designed this newsletter "to disclose information, educate the public, and provide a base of information for those individuals or organizations who wish to challenge certain practices in the West Bank."

The newsletter carries reports on al-Haq's current and previous legal interventions and on the human rights-related activities of its staff.

I&P: Israel and Palestine Political Report, **Magelan, 5 rue Cardinal Mercier, 75009 Paris, France. 6 issues/yr. Newsletter. 30 cm. 322pp. Individual subscription: $35/yr. Institutional subscription: $55/yr. Single issue: $3. Chronology, editorials, feature articles, news reports, comment and analysis, illustrations, photographs, notes.**

This hard-hitting political journal is uncompromising in its criticisms of anything and anyone that stands in the way of the goal that the editors have emblazoned in their masthead: Israel *and* Palestine. Since May 1971 this bimonthly has carried in-depth political reports and analyses of Israel and Palestine-related events in Tel Aviv, Washington, and other capitals around the world. Each issue features an "Occupation Watch" with a digest of news from more that thirty regional and international newspapers concerning the Palestinians in the Occupied Territories and Israel proper, as well as in Lebanon.

Magelan also publishes a monthly, *Report on the Palestinians under Israeli Rule* (22pp. $50/yr.), that is based essentially on news reports from Israeli and East Jerusalem media.

Israel Horizons, **Americans for Progressive Israel, 150 Fifth Ave., Rm. 911, New York, NY 10011. 6 issues/yr. Magazine. 25 cm. 32pp. Individual and institutional subscriptions: $15/yr. Single issue: $3. Feature articles, book reviews, editorials, columns, profiles, interviews, comment and analysis, letters to the editor.**

This bimonthly magazine is dedicated "to the advancement of socialist Zionism and socialism generally" and "to news and comment on the State of Israel and Jews everywhere." Its aims are "to mirror the activities of progressive forces in Israel, with the kibbutzim. . .in the vanguard."

Articles in vol. 34 (1986) fell into these categories: Israel, diaspora

Jewry, the American Jewish community, Zionism, politics (e.g., a survey of organized U.S. Jewish anti-apartheid activity), and the kibbutz movement.

Israeli Foreign Affairs, **P.O. Box 19580, Sacramento, CA 95819. 12 issues/yr. Newsletter. 28 cm. 8pp. Individual subscription: $20/yr. Institutional subscription: $35/yr. Inquire for rates outside of North America. News reports, book reviews, interviews, comment and analysis.**

The descriptive subtitle of this unique newsletter reads: "an independent monthly research report on Israel's diplomatic and military activities world wide." *Israeli Foreign Affairs* draws on a wide range of periodical and media sources to present well-documented, cogent reports on a U.S.-Israel Cooperative Development Research project in Central America, Israel's relations with Spain, the Israeli Labor Party's stand on apartheid, the testing by the U.S. Navy of Israeli "drones" (pilotless spy planes) over Nicaragua, and U.S. and West German plans to assist in the construction of diesel-powered submarines for the Israeli Navy.

Jane Hunter, *IFA*'s indefatigable publisher, also offers a monthly forty-page supplement to the newsletter with translations of articles, communications, and transcripts — some topical, others of historical value. Sample copy: US$5.

Journal of Palestine Studies: A Quarterly on Palestinian Affairs and the Arab-Israeli Conflict, **Institute for Palestine Studies, P.O. Box 25301, Georgetown Sta., Washington, DC 20007. 4 issues/yr. Magazine. 23 cm. 310pp. Individual subscription: $18/yr. Institutional subscription: $28/yr. Student rate: $16/yr. Apply for rates outside of North America. Feature articles, book reviews, documentation, interviews, notes, chronology.**

Founded in 1971, this authoritative journal has provided a forum where international specialists can discuss varying viewpoints on Palestinian affairs and the Arab-Israeli conflict. "Although the *Journal* doesn't reflect a single point of view," writes editor Hisham Sharabi, "it has a clear commitment — a commitment to fairness and dialogue." Contributors have included Maxime Rodinson, Edward Said, Zbigniew Brzezinski, Rashid Khalidi, and Ann Lesch.

In addition to substantive articles, reports, and documents, each issue of the *Journal* features these departments:

• "Arab Reports and Analysis" — a selection of research summaries and news reports from the Arabic-language press;

• "From the Israeli Press" — trends in Israel based on selections from Israeli newspapers and journals;

• "International Press" — contemporary reports on Middle Eastern affairs from outside the Arab world;

• "Recent Books" — reviews by experts of current titles in English, Arabic, and Hebrew;

• "Documents and Source Material" — documents issued by groups, organizations, and governments during the quarter;

• "Palestine Chronology" — major events dealing with social, economic, political, and military issues related to the Palestine question throughout the world;

• "Periodicals in Review" — a survey of English, French, and Arabic periodicals; and

• "Occupied Territories Report" — up-to-date analysis of the most significant events of the quarter in the West Bank and Gaza Strip.

The Link, **Americans for Middle East Understanding, 475 Riverside Dr., Rm. 771, New York, NY 10115. 6 issues/yr. Newsletter. 27 cm. 16pp. Free with membership in AMEU. Feature articles, book reviews, illustrations, photographs, notes.**

AMEU's bimonthly magazine carries one or two popularly written feature articles, plus "Book Views" and an annotated listing of Middle East-related books that are available at a discount through AMEU (see books chapter above). See chapter 5 below for descriptions of many thematic issues of *The Link* that we recommend as pamphlets.

MERIP Middle East Report, **Middle East Research and Information Project, 475 Riverside Dr., Rm. 518, New York, NY 10115. 9 issues/yr. Magazine. 27 cm. 48pp. Individual subscription: $18/yr. Institutional subscription: $34/yr. Feature articles, book reviews, editorials, documentation, interviews, letters to the editor, poetry, photographs, notes, annual index.**

This highly respected progressive magazine focuses on the political economy of the contemporary Middle East and on popular struggles in that region. This includes — in the words of the editors — "general theoretical contributions relevant to these issues and substantive articles connecting developments elsewhere in the world with the Middle East region."

As with *The Link* (above), numerous back issues of this fine publication are listed in the Pamphlets and Articles chapter below.

Middle East Insight, **International Insight, Inc., 1715 Connecticut Ave., NW, Washington, DC 20009. 6 issues/yr. Magazine. 28 cm. 48pp. Individual subscription: $25/yr. Institutional subscription: $45/yr. Feature articles, book reviews, news reports, comment and analysis, letters to the editor, photographs, notes.**

The stated aims of this bimonthly newsmagazine are: (1) to enlighten public opinion on the political, social, economic, and historical issues of the Middle East, (2) to promote better understanding between the American and the Middle Eastern people, and (3) to help search for peace in the area.

The publishing organization, International Insight, is a non-profit organization "whose purpose is to provide a spectrum of objective and insightful information on the most vital region in the world — the Middle East."

Middle East International, **Middle East International, Ltd., 21 Collingham Rd., London SW5 ONU, England. 25 issues/yr. Magazine. 29 cm. 20pp. Individual subscription: $59/yr. Institutional subscription:**

$120/yr. Library rate: $79/yr. In North America: P.O. Box 53365, Temple Heights Sta., Washington, DC 20009. Feature articles, book reviews, editorials, columnists, comment and analysis.

This authoritative, biweekly magazine offers one- and two-page-length contributions of news and commentary from *MEI* correspondents in Nicosia, Amman, Washington, D.C., Jerusalem, London, Cairo, Brussels, Damascus, and other major cities in and outside the Middle East region.

Complementing these contributions are two major articles, regular reports from the Israeli and Arabic press, column-length book reviews, and a concluding letter written from a different location around the region in each issue.

The reporting is up-to-date and accurate. The editorial stance of the magazine appears to be even-handed. Sympathy for the Palestinian cause is evident, but the leadership and tactics of Palestinian organizations are not above well-reasoned criticism.

The Middle East Journal, **Middle East Institute, 1761 N St., NW, Washington, DC 20036. 4 issues/yr. Magazine. 24 cm. 160pp. Individual and institutional subscriptions: $25/yr. Feature articles, advertisements, book reviews, essays, arts and literature, letters to the editor, notes, list of resources, chronology, bibliography of periodical literature.**

The editors of *The Middle East Journal* state that they take no editorial stand on "problems in the Middle East." Their sole criterion for submissions to the magazine, they say, is that the material published "be sound and informative and presented without emotional bias."

One-half of each issue is usually devoted to lengthy book reviews and a bibliography of periodical literature. The book reviews are arranged by country and by topics, such as social conditions, religion and philosophy, literature, economics, the Arab-Israeli conflict, and modern history and politics. The bibliography of periodical literature is noteworthy; it numbered sixteen pages in the spring 1986 issue. That same issue (vol. 40:2) contained a chronology of the Arab-Israeli conflict derived from various periodical publications, such as *Le Monde, Christian Science Monitor, Foreign Broadcast Information Service,* and the *Jerusalem Post.*

Middle East Review, **American Academic Association for Peace in the Middle East, 330 Seventh Ave., Suite 606, New York, NY 10001. 4 issues/yr. Magazine. 25 cm. 62pp. Individual and institutional subscriptions: $20/yr. Single issue: $1.50. Bulk rates available. Distributed by Transaction Periodicals Consortium (Rutgers University, New Brunswick, NJ 08903) and American Professors for Peace in the Middle East. Feature articles, advertisements, book reviews, comment and analysis, statistical tables, notes.**

The publishing organization of this journal consists of academicians who teach in colleges and universities throughout the United States. The stated purpose of the association is "to utilize the special skills and

talents of the academic community to elicit new ideas and approaches
for the solution of the Arab-Israeli conflict and to reach a just and
lasting peace in the region."

Each issue of the *Review* contains five or six academic articles devoted
to one theme, such as terrorism, oil and politics, and Israel and South
Africa. Shorter reports and a review of one or two books complete each
issue.

Middle Eastern Studies, **Frank Cass & Co., Gainsborough House, 11
Gainsborough Rd., London E11 1RS, England. 4 issues/yr. Magazine.
22 cm. 377pp. Individual subscription: £33/yr. Institutional subscription: £58/yr. Feature articles, book reviews, essays, comment and
analysis, statistical tables, notes.**

Many of the articles in this long-established academic journal are of
interest only to historians of the Middle East, e.g., "Culture and Politics
of Violence in Turkish Society, 1903–14" or "Israeli Leaders' Perceptions
of Peace, 1967–79."

Readers in areas of the world other than Europe will be particularly
interested in the journal's book reviews from British and European publishers, such as Croom Helm, Longman, Oxford University Press, and
La Découverte.

Mideast Monitor, **Association of Arab-American University Graduates, 556 Trapelo Rd., Belmont, MA 02178. 6 issues/yr. Newsletter. 28
cm. 4pp. Individual and institutional subscriptions: $10/yr. Single issue:
$2.50. Free with AAUG membership. Rates outside North America:
$13/yr. Essays, advertisements, comment and analysis, notes.**

This bimonthly bulletin of analysis and commentary on U.S. foreign
policy and Arab affairs is said to reach "American opinion- and policy-
makers, as well as church, community and human rights groups, Third
World organizations, and interested individuals in North America and
abroad."

Each issue of the *Monitor* features one essay. Examples are: "U.S.
Legal Responsibility for Israel's Violation of Palestinian Rights" by
John Quigley; "Media Hype and the Middle East" by Janice Terry; "The
Hollywood Arab: 1984–86" by Jack Shaheen; and "Israeli Strategy in
the 'Peace Process'" by Joel Beinin. Back issues of this newsletter would
make excellent group study materials for serious students of the Middle
East.

New Outlook, **9 Gordon St., Tel Aviv 63458, Israel. 12 issues/yr. 27.5
cm. 82pp. Individual subscription: $30/yr. Institutional subscription:
$41/yr. Subscribe in North America through Israel News Service, 295
Seventh Ave., New York, NY 10001.**

This influential English-language monthly was founded in 1957 "to
serve as a medium for the clarification of problems concerning peace
and cooperation among all the peoples of the Middle East." The pages
of *New Outlook* are intended to be open "to the expression of opinions,
however diverse, that have that general aim in view."

New Outlook is noteworthy for its regular coverage of the activities of peace movements and organizations in Israel, its profiles of Israeli peace activists, and its reporting on current affairs as reflected in the Arab press. Reports have appeared on the image of the Arab in the Israeli high school curriculum and the threat posed to Israeli democracy by growing extremism in the religious community.

The Other Israel, **Israeli Council for Israeli-Palestinian Peace, P.O. Box 956, Tel Aviv, Israel. 6 issues/yr. Newsletter. 25 cm. 12pp. Individual subscription: $30/yr. Institutional subscription: $50/yr. Available in North America from America-Israel Council for Israeli-Palestinian Peace. Essays, editorials, news reports, comment and analysis, letters to the editor, chronology.**

This newsletter is published to further the belief of the Israeli Council that "peace between Israel and the Palestinians is possible only on the basis of mutual recognition and that the Palestine Liberation Organization must be involved in the process." *The Other Israel* carries short reports and commentary on human rights and peace-related activities.

Palestine Focus, **November 29th Committee for Palestine, P.O. Box 27462, San Francisco, CA 94127. 6 issues/yr. Newspaper. 44 cm. 8pp. Individual subscription: $6/yr. Institutional subscription: $20/yr. First class and overseas postage rates extra. Feature articles, news reports, comment and analysis, illustrations, photographs.**

This tabloid is the national newspaper of a movement that takes its name from the date declared by the United Nations as the International Day of Solidarity with the Palestinian People. The editors describe their newspaper as "an activist vehicle tied to an activist movement, yet aimed at a general audience with little background knowledge."

The committee's statement of purpose offers a clear insight into the newspaper's content and editorial slant: "Our task," the editors write, "is to spark and support consistent, far-reaching, and effective activity which brings the issue of Palestine before the American people and builds a growing and deepening base of understanding. Our committee organizes to stop U.S. intervention in the Middle East and to cut off U.S. aid to Israel. We educate Americans on the need to support the Palestine Liberation Organization, which is the sole legitimate representative of the Palestinian people, and to oppose Israeli policies of discrimination which deny the Palestinian people their rights."

Palestine Human Rights Newsletter, **Palestine Human Rights Campaign, 220 S. State St., Suite 1308, Chicago, IL 60604. 6 issues/yr. Newsletter. 28 cm. 16pp. Individual and institutional subscriptions: $12/yr. PHRC special reports are included in subscription fee. News reports, editorials, documentation, comment and analysis, illustrations, photographs, chronology.**

This newsletter, which began its seventh year of publication in 1987, carries news and commentary in line with the aims of the Palestine Human Rights Campaign: "to secure internationally recognized human rights for the Palestinian people" and to lend "all possible support" to members of the Palestinian community whose rights have been violated.

The campaign itself is composed of individuals drawn from religious, academic, civil rights, and peace communities. The newsletter would appeal to just that audience.

Palestine Perspectives, **Palestine Research and Educational Center, 2025 Eye St., NW, Suite 415, Washington, DC 20006. 6 issues/yr. Magazine. 28 cm. 16pp. Individual and institutional subscriptions: $15/yr. Feature articles, book reviews, editorials, documentation, news reports, essays.**

Regular sections in this polished publication of the PREC include "PLO News and Views," "Life under Occupation," "Washington Watch," and "World View." Each issue contains two or three brief original essays or reprinted articles from the U.S. press.

The Search: Journal for Arab and Islamic Studies, **Center for Arab and Islamic Studies, P.O. Box 543, Brattleboro, VT 05301. 4 issues/yr. Magazine. 21 cm. 166pp. Individual subscription: $15/yr. Institutional subscription: $25/yr. Student rate: $12/yr. Feature articles, advertisements, notes.**

This journal reflects the purposes of the Center for Arab and Islamic Studies, which is dedicated "to the advancement of education, particularly for the promotion of understanding, communication, and friendship among the American and Arab-Islamic peoples." The center publishes *The Search* in order to inform its American audience of cultural, economic, and political affairs related to the Arab-Islamic peoples.

Many articles in this journal are quite restricted in their focus and would be of interest only to scholars. "Emphasis Assimilation in Classical Arabic" by Dr. Mohamed Al-Shorafat is such an example. Other articles would appeal to the average reader, for example, "Israel's Strategy for the American Campus: A Threat to Academic Freedom?" by Naseer H. Aruri or "Algeria and Libya and the Palestinian Question" by Saadallah A. S. Hallaba.

Shalom: Jewish Peace Letter, **Jewish Peace Fellowship, P.O. Box 271, Nyack, NY 10960. 4 issues/yr. Newsletter. 28 cm. 8pp. Individual and institutional subscriptions: $5/yr. Essays, book reviews, news reports, network news.**

"The problem of peace has never penetrated the consciousness of the Jewish community to a sufficient degree," writes Elie Weisel, 1986 Nobel Laureate for Peace, in the fall 1986 edition of *Shalom.* "And I mean not only peace in Israel, which we all desire," Weisel continues, "but peace everywhere. Why not? I confess to you, I don't have the answer."

Ironic that Weisel's provocative statement should be published in the newsletter of a Jewish peace organization that has been trying its best to penetrate the consciousness of the Jewish community with peace-related news for more than twenty years. The editors of *Shalom* acknowledge the truth in Weisel's observation and accept his statement not as a criticism but as a challenge to redouble their efforts.

Issues of *Shalom* chronicle the work of the Jewish Peace Fellowship in relation to the Middle East and to other troubled parts of the globe. Peace activists in other religious communities will want to monitor this newsletter in order to broaden their understanding of the issues and of action possibilities in pursuit of peace.

Tikkun: A Quarterly Jewish Critique of Politics, Culture & Society, Institute for Labor and Mental Health, 5100 Leona St., Oakland, CA 94619. 4 issues/yr. Magazine. 27 cm. 124pp. Individual subscription: $20/yr. Institutional subscription: $45/yr. Feature articles, advertisements, book reviews, editorials, comment and analysis.

Though not focused specifically on the Middle East, this magazine, launched in 1986, is noteworthy for the window it provides on the liberal and progressive Jewish intellectual community in the United States. According to its editors, *Tikkun* presents "intellectually sophisticated analyses of politics and culture, history and philosophy, social theory and psychoanalysis, literary criticism and Judaica." The magazine is addressed — and will appeal most — to policy makers and community activists, intellectuals and people "who wish to shape our common destiny." ("Tikkun" means to "mend, repair, and transform the world.")

The premiere issue of *Tikkun* featured articles on the New Right, the sources of democratic change, and a new anti-nuclear strategy, in addition to a symposium entitled, "What Kind of Tikkun Does the World Need?"

Washington Report on Middle East Affairs, American Educational Trust, P.O. Box 53062, Washington, DC 20009. 12 issues/yr. Newsletter. 28 cm. 24pp. Individual subscription: $25/yr. Institutional subscription: $50/yr. Single issue: $1. Essays, book reviews, documentation, news reports, comment and analysis, illustrations.

The subtitle on this publication, "A Survey of United States Relations with Middle East Countries," reflects the preoccupation of the magazine's publishers, the American Educational Trust, with critical assessment of U.S. involvement in the Middle East. This preoccupation is further refined by the location of the AET offices in Washington, D.C., and by the in-field experience that former U.S. foreign service personnel bring to their contributions to the newsletter (as editors and writers). The editors' concerns with the shaping of U.S. foreign policy — at all levels of the U.S. government — is plain to see in the *Report*. This is the strength of this well-written and attractively designed newsletter.

AET performs a valuable service by providing an eight-page annotated catalog of books, monographs, films, and information services in each issue of the *Washington Report*. These materials can be ordered directly from AET at discounted prices.

AET also distributes two substantial weekly publications: (1) *The Middle East Clipboard,* 150 clippings selected from the *Jerusalem Post* and leading U.S., Arab, and British dailies and periodicals, and (2) *The Middle East Times,* a weekly newspaper published in Nicosia, Turkey.

SUPPLEMENTARY LIST OF PERIODICALS

ADC Reports, American-Arab Anti-Discrimination Committee, 1731 Connecticut Ave., NW, Suite 400, Washington, DC 20009. Magazine. 28 cm. 50pp. Free with ADC membership.

ADC Times, American-Arab Anti-Discrimination Committee, 1731 Connecticut Ave., NW, Washington, DC 20009. 10 issues/yr. 28 cm. 16pp. Free with ADC membership.

Arab Perspectives, Arab Information Center, 1100 17 St., NW, Suite 901, Washington, DC 20036. 12 issues/yr. Magazine. 20.5 cm. 78pp. Individual and institutional subscriptions: $10/yr. Student rate: $6/yr.

CAFIOT Newsletter, Committee for Academic Freedom in the Occupied Territories, 300 Eshelman Hall, University of California, Berkeley, CA 94720. 12 issues/yr. Newsletter.

Contemporary Mideast Backgrounder, Media Analysis Center, P.O. Box 13169, Jerusalem 91131. 52 issues/yr.

Crescent International, 300 Steelcase Rd. W., Unit 8, Markham, Ontario L3R 2W2, England. 26 issues/yr.

The Dialogue, American Coalition for Middle East Dialogue, Stony Point Center, Stony Point, NY 10980. 4 issues/yr. Newsletter. 28 cm. 4pp. Free with membership.

Free Palestine, P.O. Box 492, London SW19 4PJ, England. 12 issues/yr.

Gazelle Review of Literature on the Middle East, Ithaca Press, 13 Southwark St., London SE1, England. 2 issues/yr. Magazine. Single issue: $5.50, postage included.

Genesis 2, Rebirth 2, Inc., 99 Bishop Allen Dr., Cambridge, MA 02139. 6 issues/yr. Magazine. 28 cm. 40pp. Individual subscription: $15/yr. Institutional subscription: $20/yr.

International Journal of Middle East Studies, Cambridge University Press, 32 E. 57 St., New York, NY 10022. 4 issues/yr. Magazine. 18 cm. Individual and institutional subscriptions: $84/yr.

Iran Times, 2727 Wisconsin Ave., NW, Washington, DC 20007. 52 issues/yr.

Islamic Quarterly, The Islamic Cultural Centre, 146 Park Rd., London NW8, England. 4 issues/yr.

Israel Press Briefs, International Center for Peace in the Middle East, 107 Hahashmonaim St., Tel Aviv 67011, Israel. Newsletter. 23.5 cm.

Israel Weekly News Review, 6 Hamajid St., Tel Aviv 65224, Israel. 52 issues/yr. Magazine.

Israeleft, P.O. Box 9013, Jerusalem 91-090, Israel. 24 issues/yr.

Israeli-Palestinian Peace Newsletter, P.O. Box 4991, Washington, DC 20008. Newsletter.

Jewish Currents, 22 E. 17 St., Rm. 601, New York, NY 10003. 12 issues/yr.

Journal of Arab Affairs, 7872 Fairview Rd., Boulder, CO 80303. 2 issues/yr. Magazine. 21 cm. 110pp. Individual and institutional subscriptions: $25/yr.

Journal of Near Eastern Studies, University of Chicago, 1155 E. 58 St., Chicago, IL 60637. 4 issues/yr. Magazine.

Journal of South Asian and Middle Eastern Studies, Pakistan American Foundation, 138 Tolentine Hall, Villanova University, Villanova, PA 19085. 4 issues/yr. Magazine. 15 cm. 96pp. Individual subscription: $20/yr. Institutional subscription: $25/yr. Rates outside of North America: $30/yr.

Khamsin: Journal of Revolutionary Socialists of the Middle East, Ithaca Press, 13 Southwark St., London SE1 1RQ, England. 4 issues/yr. Magazine. 22 cm. Single issue: $3.50.

The Maghreb Review, London WC1N 1AG, England. 6 issues/yr.

MELA Notes, Middle East Librarians' Association, University of Chicago Library, Rm. 560, Chicago, IL 60637. 3 issues/yr. Newsletter.

The Middle East, Magazines Ltd., 63 Long Acre, London WC2E 9JH, England. 12 issues/yr. Magazine.

Middle East Economic Digest, MEED Ltd., 21 John St., London WC 17 1BP, England. 52 issues/yr. Magazine.

Middle East Focus, Association of Arab-American University Graduates, 556 Trapelo Rd., Belmont, MA 02178. 12 issues/yr. Newsletter.

Middle East Magazine, IC Publications Ltd., 69 Great Queen St., London WC2B 5BN, England. 12 issues/yr. Magazine.

Middle East Notebook, National Committee for Middle East Studies, 823 United Nations Plaza, New York, NY 10017. 4 issues/yr. 28 cm.

Middle East Perspective: A Newsletter on Eastern Mediterranean and North African Affairs, P.O. Box 154, Springfield, VA 22150. 11 issues/yr. Magazine.

Middle East Review, World of Information, 21 Gold St., Saffron, Walden, Essex CB10 1EJ, England. 1 issue/yr.

Middle East Studies Association Bulletin, University of Arizona, Tucson, AZ 85721. 2 issues/yr.

Mideast Observer in Washington, Development Associates, 2924 Columbia Pike, Arlington, VA 22204. 20 issues/yr. Newsletter. 28 cm. 4pp. Individual subscription: $47/yr. Institutional subscription: $100/yr. Single issue: $2.

Mideast Press Report, Claremont Research and Publications, 160 Claremont Ave., New York, NY 10027. 52 issues/yr.

Mideast Report, 60 E. 42 St., Suite 1433, New York, NY 10017.

Muslim World, 77 Sherman St., Hartford, CT 06105. 4 issues/yr.

The Muslim World League Journal, Muslim World League, P.O. Box 537, Mecca al-Mukarramah, Saudi Arabia. 12 issues/yr.

Near East Report, 500 N. Capitol St., NW, Washington, DC 20001. 52 issues/yr.

The Palestine Review, 1884 Columbia Rd., NW, Washington, DC 20009. 12 issues/yr. Magazine.

PCNA Monthly, Palestine Congress of North America, P.O. Box 9621, Washington, DC 20016. 12 issues/yr. Newspaper. 38.5 cm. 12pp.

Shdemot: Cultural Forum of the Kibbutz Movement, 10 Dubnow St., Tel Aviv, Israel. 4 issues/yr. Magazine. Individual subscription: $12/yr. Institutional subscription: $15/yr. Specify English-language version. Bimonthly Hebrew edition also available.

Shmate: A Journal of Progressive Jewish Thought, Shmate, P.O. Box 4228, Berkeley, CA 94704. 4 issues/yr. Magazine. 27.5 cm. 28pp. Individual subscription: $15/yr. Institutional subscription: $25/yr. Single issue: $4.

INFORMATION SOURCES

For information on establishment news magazines and academic journals with Middle East coverage we suggest that you consult the bibliographies, guides, and reference books described in chapter 2 above. See, in particular, the regular surveys of periodical literature in magazines such as *The Middle East Journal* and the *Journal of Palestine Studies*. Standard library reference guides, such as *The IMS Ayer Directory of Publications, The Serials Directory: An International Reference Book,* and *Ulrich's International Periodicals Directory,* should also be consulted.

The spring 1987 issue of *Third World Resources* listed and described numerous reference guides that contain information on Middle East-related periodicals; these reference works include the *Directory of Development Education Periodicals* and the *Oxbridge Directory of Ethnic Periodicals* (50 cents, from Third World Resources, 464 19 St., Oakland, CA 94612). See the publications from **Third World Resources,** described in the preface to this resource directory.

4

Pamphlets and Articles

The aim of this chapter is to present printed resource materials that are self-contained (usually an entire issue of a magazine on one topic), brief, inexpensive, and easily available, often at bulkrates.

The dividing line between a book and a pamphlet (or booklet) is a thin one at times. The rule of thumb used to distinguish between the two was: bound, printed materials that numbered less than one hundred pages, were priced at less than $5, or were one volume of a serial publication are listed in the pamphlets and articles chapter. Admittedly this dividing line is arbitrary, and it is hoped that no author will be offended that her/his work is classed as a "pamphlet." Resources in this chapter are no less important because they are concise.

This chapter is divided into three parts: annotated entries, supplementary list of pamphlets and articles, and sources of additional information on pamphlets and articles.

Information in the **annotated entries** is given in the following order: author(s) or editor(s); title; publisher; periodical name; publication data (volume, number, date); number of pages; price; keyword description of format; and description of content.

Pamphlets and articles in the **supplementary list** (pp. 92–95) are grouped under these headings: Middle East general; Arabian Peninsula and the Gulf; Fertile Crescent; North Africa; Iran; and Turkey. Information in the entries in this part is given in the following order: author(s) or editor(s); title; publisher; name of periodical; publication data; number of pages; and price.

The part entitled **information sources** (p. 96) provides information about directories and guides that contain the names of other articles and pamphlets related to the Middle East.

The titles of all the entries in this chapter are integrated into the titles index at the back of the directory. See the organizations index for addresses of publishers or distributors that appear in this chapter. (Note that whenever the names of the publisher and the periodical are identical, the names will appear in both the titles and organizations indexes.)

ANNOTATED ENTRIES

Ahmad, Eqbal, et al. *Terrorism and Intervention.* **Middle East Research and Information Project.** *MERIP Middle East Report* 16, no. 3 (May-June 1986). 48pp. $3.50. Notes, interview, photographs.

This fifteenth anniversary issue of the *Middle East Report* opens with a provocative essay by Eqbal Ahmad on the nature and practice of terrorism during the last four centuries. Ahmad illustrates how judgments about terrorism are usually skewed in favor of the ruling powers. "Official" terrorism, such as Israeli air attacks on civilian targets in Lebanon, is condoned or explained away, while the terrorist acts of stateless peoples such as the Palestinians are given heightened attention in the press.

Editor Joe Stork follows with an analysis of the April 1986 U.S. attack on Libya. He examines the Reagan Administration's obsessive desire to "get Qaddafi" and situates U.S.-Libya relations in a regional context. An interview with Noam Chomsky on "the first prime time bombing in history" picks up the same theme. Chomsky explains why "terrorism" is such a useful ideological construct for proponents of U.S. military intervention. He concludes with a brief statement on Washington's use of a highly militarized Israel to further its foreign policy aims in Central America and South Africa.

Cheryl Rubenberg develops this critical understanding of Israel's global role in her article on "Israel and Guatemala: Arms, Aid and Counterinsurgency." Milton Jamail and Margo Gutierrez do the same in their study of "Israel in Central America: Nicaragua, Honduras, El Salvador, Costa Rica."

This issue of the *Middle East Report* also contains a review essay by Fred Halliday of two books that deal with the "Reagan Doctrine" and Iran.

Aruri, Naseer. *The Middle East on the U.S. Campus.* **Americans for Middle East Understanding.** *The Link* 18, no. 2 (May-June 1985). 16pp. $2.50. Notes, photographs.

The Johns Hopkins School of Advanced International Studies in Washington, D.C., started the first Middle East study center in the United States in 1946. Today some seventeen major Middle East Centers are functioning at universities and colleges and more than a hundred institutions of higher learning offer Middle East area courses.

Naseer Aruri, a professor of political science at Southeastern Massachusetts University, describes in this article some of the ways in which teachers' academic freedom is violated; in particular he emphasizes instances in which academics have been called "pro-Arab propagandists" or have been accused of using "their anti-Zionism as merely a guise for their deeply felt anti-Semitism."

The article surveys the premises, implications, and techniques—surveillance, monitoring, and intelligence gathering—of this "new offensive." Aruri briefly describes several cases in which charges of anti-Semitism were brought against individual professors or organizations and the way in which Middle East Studies Centers have become suspect.

Aruri believes that the campaign to stifle criticism of Israeli policies on American campuses can only result in increasing intolerance and in a weakening of civil liberties for all.

Aruri, Naseer, Fouad Moughrabi, and Joe Stork. *Reagan and the Middle East.* **Association of Arab-American University Graduates.** *Monograph* **no. 17, 1983. 95pp. $5.50. Notes, figures, statistical tables, appendixes, documents.**

Three essays provide a comprehensive analysis of the Reagan Administration's Middle East peace plan, its context, objectives, and projected consequences. Aruri, Moughrabi, and Stork examine, in particular, the key part played by Israel in the U.S. Middle East strategy and the secondary role that has been assigned to Washington's Arab allies in the region.

The appendixes contain the text of President Reagan's policy-setting speech on the Middle East in September 1982, the Israeli Cabinet's communiqué on the Reagan Administration's Middle East proposals, and excerpts from the official English-language text of the final declaration issued by the Arab summit at Fez, Morocco, on September 9, 1982.

Awad, Mubarak E., and R. Scott Kennedy. *Nonviolent Struggle in the Middle East.* **New Society Publishers. 1985. 40pp. $2.95. Notes, photographs.**

Tuo reprints from 1984 editions of the *Journal of Palestine Studies* are reproduced in this booklet: "The Druze of the Golan: A Case of Nonviolent Resistance" by R. Scott Kennedy, an American peace activist with a good deal of experience in the Middle East, and "Nonviolent Resistance: A Strategy for the Occupied Territories" by Mubarak E. Awad, a Palestinian psychologist who founded the Palestine Center for the Study of Nonviolence in Jerusalem.

Scott Kennedy describes how the Druze — "a tight-knit, fiercely independent, politically flexible and pragmatic, and sometimes militant force in Middle Eastern politics" — waged a 'courageous and effective' nonviolent campaign in the Syrian Golan Heights against the Israeli occupation in 1982. "In a region and a conflict sick with violence," he writes, "the Golani Druze demonstrated the efficacy and power of nonviolence as a method of social struggle which can be utilized by unarmed civilians confronted by overwhelming police and military force."

Side by side with armed struggle, writes the author of the second article in this booklet, "Palestinians have used non-violent methods since the beginning of the 1930s. . .in their attempts to achieve their goals against Zionism." Mubarak Awad outlines the history of this nonviolent movement and weighs its applicability as a strategy for those suffering under Israeli military occupation on the West Bank.

Ball, George W. *Why Was Flight 847 Skyjacked?* **Americans for Middle East Understanding.** *AMEU Public Affairs Series,* **no. 26, 1986. 20pp.**

This sympathetic, well-reasoned, and courageous examination by a seasoned statesman and diplomat of the causes of the skyjacking of TWA flight 847 in 1985 challenges readers to "come to grips with the central issue of motivation in the context of history and of larger policy." Ball urges us to get beyond our initial rush of feelings and all the media hype and seriously analyze why a group of Lebanese Shias would murder one American and hold 152 others hostage for two weeks.

Ball is forthright in his condemnation of Washington's "automatic support of Israeli projects and ambitions even when they contravened U.S. interests."

His revelations about the Israeli/U.S. policies and actions that gave rise to the skyjacking are as enlightening as they are provocative.

Beinin, Joel, et al. *Egypt and Israel Today.* Middle East Research and Information Project. *MERIP Reports* 14, no. 1 (Jan. 1985). 32pp. $2.75. Notes, photographs, statistical tables.

March 26, 1985, marked the sixth anniversary of the "Camp David" peace treaty between Egypt and Israel. This issue of the *MERIP Reports* asks: "What have been the consequences of this pact, and where is the peace it was supposed to usher into the region?"

Stanford University history professor Joel Beinin opens this issue with a detailed study of the two separate "frameworks" for agreements that were contained in the Camp David Accords. The first, a strictly bilateral arrangement between Egypt and Israel, mandated the full Israeli withdrawal from the territories occupied in the 1967 war. The second element provided for negotiations among Egypt, Israel, Jordan, and Palestinian representatives over the future of the West Bank and the Gaza Strip. While the first element in the Camp David Accords was all but completely implemented, Beinin states, little if any action has been taken on the second and the "Camp David process" has become "hopelessly stalled." In his seven-page article Beinin searches for the reasons why.

Two substantive articles complete this study of Egypt and Israel: University of Amsterdam anthropology professor Bertus Hendriks contributes an eight-page analysis of the May 1984 general elections in Egypt and Hebrew University professor Zvi Schuldiner analyzes the "national unity" cabinet that the Israeli government installed after the 1984 elections for the eleventh Knesset.

Beinin, Joel, et al. *West Bank, Gaza, Israel: Marching toward Civil War.* Middle East Research and Information Project. *MERIP Reports* 15, nos. 8–9 (Oct.-Dec. 1985). 64pp. $4.50. Notes, photographs, interviews, documents, list of resources.

This special double issue of *MERIP Reports* documents the escalation of violence and tension in the occupied territories in 1985 and traces the growth of the Israeli "settler movement" and its most militant wing, the "Jewish terrorist underground."

Joel Beinin sets the tone for this issue in his opening article: "In an article written in early 1985," he says, "Ze'ev Schiff described the Palestinian and Jewish populations of Israel and the occupied territories as 'marching, . . . toward a civil war.'" "Since then," Beinin says, "events have only confirmed the accuracy of Schiff's observation." Beinin describes the ongoing acts of violence—noting especially the role of Meir Kahane's Jewish Defense League in instigating racist attacks against Palestinians in the occupied territories.

In the next article in this issue, Joan Mandell writes from her years of experience in Gaza about conditions in the "ghetto territory" that she aptly characterizes as "Israel's Soweto." Shlomo Frenkel, economics editor of the Israeli daily newspaper *Hadashot,* follows with an analysis of "Israel's Economic Crisis." Frenkel explains how U.S. military aid signals Washington's approval of Israeli policies in the West Bank and Gaza at the same time as which it subsidizes the U.S. weapons industry and further militarizes the Israeli economy. Joost Hiltermann describes the emerging trade union movement in the West Bank and chronicles the numerous Israeli military attacks against Palestinian political and trade union leaders.

Beit-Hallahmi, Benjamin. *U.S.-Israeli-Central American Connection.* **Americans for Middle East Understanding.** *The Link* **18, no. 4 (Nov. 1985). 16pp. $2.50. Map, photographs, notes.**

Israeli Professor Benjamin Beit-Hallahmi, an authority on Israel's involvement in the third world, documents Israeli involvement in Central America in this article. He shows the extent to which and why Israel is the U.S. proxy in that troubled region.

Guatemala, El Salvador, Honduras, Costa Rica, and Nicaragua (the Somozas and the Contras) are examined in turn. Beit-Hallahmi sees Israel's growing involvement in Central America since 1975 as a collaborative venture with the United States. He tracks the history of Israel's contributions to Central American regimes—principally in furnishing arms and advisors—and points to the role of Israel in the region as "the arm of the United States."

Brownlee, William H. *Israel and the Ten Commandments: An Appeal to the Conscience Based upon the Modern History of Palestine.* **Americans for Middle East Understanding.** *AMEU Public Affairs Series* **no. 24, 1984. 78pp. Notes.**

This "outpouring of moral concerns over the Holy Land" is a well-reasoned, scripturally sound examination of Israel's conduct as measured against each of the Ten Commandmants. "As a Biblical scholar and a student of the Holy Land," writes Dr. William Hugh Brownlee, "I am a great admirer of the Jews for their spiritual and intellectual achievements, past and present; but I am grieved by modern materialism and militarism which today distort and obscure these great achievements of the Jews."

"The greatest contribution of Judaism to universal morality is no doubt the Ten Commandments," Brownlee continues, "as these have greatly influenced not only the great monotheistic religions but civil law as well." He acknowledges that the actions of all nations would be found wanting "or only relatively good" when measured against these commandments. But Brownlee believes that Israel must be held to an even higher standard because of the Zionist claim that Judaism is both a religion and a nation — "that nationhood is inseparable from Judaism as a religion." "This means that the state of Israel must meet especially severe standards," Brownlee concludes, "if it is to warrant a major place in the religion of Judaism."

Thus Brownlee launches this critical assessment of Israel's public behavior. He begins with the commandment "Thou shalt not covet" and works his way back — chapter-by-chapter — to the first commandment, "I am the Lord thy God."

Church groups would find this treatise particularly revealing.

Cooper, Roger. *The Baha'is of Iran*. Minority Rights Group. *MRG Report*, no. 51, 1985. Rev. ed. 16pp. $3.95. Notes, documentation, photographs, maps, bibliography, appendix.

"This report has been prepared at a time when Baha'is in Iran are suffering on a scale unprecedented in this century," writes Middle East specialist Roger Cooper. This Minority Rights Group pamphlet explains who the Baha'is are and why they are being persecuted for their faith by the Iranian government of Ayatollah Khomeini.

The Baha'is of Iran traces the development of the Baha'i faith from its origins in the mid-nineteenth century to its extension today to more than two hundred countries and territories. Of the more than three million Baha'is worldwide, some three hundred thousand live in Iran. Roger Cooper marshalls plenty of evidence to document the wholesale — and official — violation of the human rights of the Baha'is in Iran by the fundamentalist Islamic government that wrested power from the Shah in 1979. Baha'is are not recognized as a religious minority under the New Islamic Constitution, although they are the largest religious minority in Iran. They are denied full rights as citizens and their beliefs are villified in the state-controlled media. Cooper estimates that close to two hundred Baha'is have been executed or otherwise murdered for their beliefs from the start of the Islamic Revolution (late 1978) to mid-March 1985. Many of these and others have been severely tortured in an effort to get them to recant their faith.

This booklet closes with a report on the international reaction to the persecution of Baha'is in Iran and a summary of events since the first appearance of *The Baha'is of Iran* in February 1982.

Davis, Nira Yuval. *Israeli Women and Men. Change International Report*, 1984. 23pp. $3. Available from Women's International Resource Exchange Service. Maps, tables, bibliography.

In this reprint from *Change International Report,* Nira Davis, an Israeli, challenges the many myths attached to Israel and to Israeli women in particular; her essay is a penetrating scrutiny of women's realities on many levels: the sexual division of labor on the kibbutz, past and present, as well as in urban work centers; the gender-determined duration and direction of study; official policies and ideological pressure to reproduce; motherhood as the primary duty of women; secular and religious laws and their maternity-oriented definitions of women; the women's army corp, Chen (Charm), and the "illusion of equality" in the armed forces; and, finally, participation in political parties, trade unions, and government posts.

"Either a Veil or a Beat on the Head": Repression and Response of Women in Iran. **Women's International Resource Exchange Service. 18pp. $1.80. Graphics, photographs, notes.**

This booklet contains three reprinted reports on the situation of women in Iran: (1) "Women and Struggle in Iran," a document from the Iranian Student Association (summer 1984); (2) "Women, State and Ideology in Iran," by Haleh Afshar (*Third World Quarterly,* April 1985); and "The Women's Movement in Iran: A Hopeful Prognosis, by Azar Tabari (*Feminist Studies* 12, no. 2 [summer 1986]).

These three accounts describe the conditions of women under the Shah's regime and document the role women played in his downfall. They also describe the subsequent events and policies of the new government that have brought about continued repression of women's rights, including impoverishment, death, and exile for many women and pulic harassment, ridicule, and quasi-prostitution for women left widowed by the war with Iraq.

Azar Tabari's article analyzes the potential for a women's movement in Iran and describes the key role it can play in building resistance to the Islamic state.

Dearden, Ann, ed. *Arab Women.* **Minority Rights Group.** *MRG Report,* **no. 27, 1983. Rev. ed. 16pp. $4. Notes, maps, statistical tables, bibliography, chronology.**

Journalist and author Ann Dearden introduces this survey of the role and status of Arab women by cautioning that Arab women cannot be easily classified. True, among all of the world's Muslim women, Dearden says, "they form a distinctive group." But their status varies greatly, the author notes, "according to the country they live in and section of society to which they belong."

With this caution in mind editor Dearden has organized this regional survey on a country-by-country basis. Dearden's brief historical and regional overview is followed by contributed essays on Arab women in Egypt, Lebanon, Syria, Iraq, Tunisia, Algeria, Saudi Arabia, the People's Democratic Republic of Yemen (South Yemen), the United Arab Emirates, and Oman. The final section on "Other Countries" includes paragraph-length reports on Palestinian women and on Arab women in Sudan, Libya, Kuwait, Bahrain, Qatar, the Yemen Arab Republic (North Yemen), Morocco, and Jordan.

Editor Dearden updates the original survey by describing the position of Arab women in 1983. *Arab Women* concludes with a bibliography of twenty-two books on this subject and a page of charts and a table of census statistics for the region.

Hagopian, Elaine C., ed. *Amal and the Palestinians: Understanding the Battle of the Camps.* **Association of Arab-American University Graduates.** *Occasional Paper* **no. 9, 1985. 33pp. $4. Chronology, documents, appendix.**

The two essays in this pamphlet, one by Naseer Aruri and the other by As'ad Abu Khalil, examine the ways in which the present Syrian leadership sought to gain influence over the Palestine Liberation Organization in the years following the Israeli invasion of Lebanon in 1982. In her introduction, Elaine Hagopian explains how "in the aftermath of the [1982] war, Syria was able to take advantage of the discontent within the PLO and supported the dissidents within its ranks." "The Syrian-supported Lebanese Amal militia," she says, "continued, in the May-June 1985 battle of the camps in Beirut, to try to reduce the remaining PLO structure in Lebanon. It did not succeed."

One-half of this booklet is given to a descriptive chronology of events and full-text accounts from British and U.S. newspapers.

Hallaj, Muhammad. *From Time Immemorial: The Resurrection of a Myth.* **Americans for Middle East Understanding.** *The Link* **18, no. 1 (Jan.-March 1985). 16pp. $2.50. Notes, photographs.**

From Time Immemorial: The Origins of the Arab-Jewish Conflict Over Palestine, the 1984 book by U.S. writer Joan Peters, has been labeled by one reviewer, Norman Finkelstein, as being "among the most spectacular frauds ever published on the Arab-Israeli conflict."

In "The Resurrection of a Myth" Dr. Muhammad Hallaj critically examines the arguments advanced by Peters and reaches a similar conclusion. He characterizes the 412 pages of her text and 120 pages of footnotes as a "collection of errors, distortions, fallacies and even obvious inventions and fabrications."

"The overall purpose of *From Time Immemorial,* Hallaj states, "is to deny that the Palestinians have rights or valid claims in Palestine or that the Zionist movement had committed any transgression against them." "What Joan Peters claims to show," Hallaj continues, "is that Palestine, especially the parts which later became the state of Israel, was desolate and abandoned before Zionist colonization revived the land and attracted Arab immigrants. Therefore, the Palestinians have no right to claim that they were dispossessed and displaced by the establishment of a Jewish state in Palestine in 1948. This is the crux of her argument," Hallaj concludes.

Muhammad Hallaj exposes three of the myths that Peters presents to her readers as established facts: (1) the myth of land without people; (2) the myth of neglected land; and (3) the myth of the happy natives. "The Resurrection of a Myth" is a powerful antidote to Peters's influential work.

Hallaj, Muhammad. *Israel's West Bank Gamble.* **General Union of Palestinian Students USA.** *Information Papers Series,* **no. 2, December 1986. 24pp. $1. Notes, interviews, review essay, book reviews, recommended readings, photographs, maps, bibliography.**

In this article, reprinted from the summer 1984 issue of *American-Arab Affairs,* Dr. Muhammad Hallaj makes the point that Israel's policy toward the West Bank and Gaza, the Palestinian territories Israel seized in 1967, "is not only inimical to Palestinian rights but also detrimental to peace in the Middle East." Hallaj's central argument is that

"Israel's policy is undermining the most promising gains made in the politics of the Arab-Israeli conflict since it began, by altering the nature and scope of the conflict from one between Israel and the Arabs over the West Bank and Gaza to an Arab-Zionist struggle over Palestine."

The author, the director of the Palestine Research and Educational Center in Washington, D.C., concludes by saying that "the most constructive international act which may be possible at the moment is to dissuade Israel from continuing with its policy of 'creating facts' [that is, establishing settlements in the occupied territories], which may make the reconciliation of Arab and Israeli positions impractical without major dislocations in the region."

Washington's "continued refusal to recognize the Palestinian's rights to independence," Hallaj charges, ". . .its continued refusal to recognize the PLO, and its continued efforts to shelter Israel's policy in the West Bank and Gaza against international sanctions, send the wrong signals to Israel and encourage it in the mistaken belief that the 'final solution' it seeks to the Palestinian question is indeed achievable."

Halliday, Fred, et al. *The Contest for Arabia*. Middle East Research and Information Project. *MERIP Reports* 15, no. 2 (Feb. 1985). 32pp. $2.75. Notes, photographs, maps, chronology.

Fred Halliday, author of *Arabia without Sultans* (London: Pelican, 1974), contributed the opening article, "North Yemen Today," to this MERIP report on the Arabian Peninsula. Halliday, who teaches at the London School of Economics and is a frequent visitor to the Middle East, writes that "commercial capitalism is alive and well" in this little-known country on the southeastern tip of the peninsula. He adds, however, that the well-being of North Yemen's economy is very dependent on remittances of Yemeni emigrants and on foreign aid. In his seven-page article Halliday weighs the impact of this dependency on North Yemen's development. He describes, as well, the political realities that have shaped the Yemen Arab Republic.

K. Celine offers a short report on a January 1985 visit to Kuwait, and the editors of the *MERIP Reports* provide a brief survey article on opposition movements in the Arabian Peninsula. Interviews with two representatives of peninsula opposition organizations (one from the Yemen Arab Republic and the other from Saudi Arabia) and a review essay by *Washington Post* reporter Scott Armstrong entitled "The Gulf between the Superpowers" bring this issue to a close.

Hélie-Lucas, Marie Aimée. *Bound and Gagged by the Family Code*. *Trouble and Strife*, 1985. 8pp. $1.20. Available from Women's International Resource Exchange Service. Photographs.

In an interview with Sophie Laws, Hélie-Lucas explains the Algerian family code (the Law on Personal Status) and gives examples of the code's impact on women: women are given in marriage by a man of their own family, the stated aim of marriage is reproduction, infertility is grounds for "repudiation," only men may file for divorce, and women must have permission from fathers or husbands in order to work. Among other issues covered are the problems of unwed mothers and abandoned children, the taboo on premarital sex, and the question of state-controlled rights to sterilization, abortion, and contraception.

Hiltermann, Joost R. *Al-Haq's Response to the Chapter on Israel and the Occupied Territories in the U.S. State Department's "Country Reports on Human Rights Practices for 1984."* **Al-Haq/Law in the Service of Man. December 1986. 18pp.**

Each year Al-Haq, Law in the Service of Man, studies carefully and responds critically to the chapter in the annual U.S. State Department report dealing with the human rights situation in Israel and the Occupied Territories.

Al-Haq's reply, written in early 1985, to the 1984 State Department report is reproduced in full in this pamphlet. The report points to a number of distortions and omissions serious enough to undermine the report's value. This Al-Haq report has been published not primarily to point out specific errors but rather to "place the errors in their conceptual context: Why were such errors permitted to recur over and again? And why did Al-Haq's previous critique, and critiques provided by other parties, have so little impact on the accuracy of subsequent State Department reports, or — in light of Israel's record in the area of human rights, described in these reports — on the continued high level of U.S. economic and military aid to Israel in general?"

The report concludes that the State Department report on human rights in the Israeli-occupied West Bank and Gaza can only be read with skepticism and recommends other documentation on human rights violations there (such as that published by Amnesty International, the International Commission of Jurists, the National Lawyers Guild, and the International Association of Democratic Lawyers) for "concerned parties."

Hooglund, Eric, et al. *The Middle East: Living by the Sword.* **Middle East Research and Information Project.** *MERIP Middle East Report* **17, no. 1 (Jan.-Feb. 1987). 48pp. $3.50. Notes, tables, photographs, document, maps, chronology.**

"Revelations about secret talks and arms deals between the United States and Iran have focused attention on the internal politics of the Islamic Republic," writes Eric Hooglund in his opening essay, "The Search for Iran's 'Moderates'." Hooglund's description of the political forces within Iran and all of the other articles in this excellent issue of the *Middle East Report* are essential background reading for the Middle Eastern aspect of the "Iran-contra" affair.

Articles in this issue are: "Iran's Grand New Strategy" by Fred Halliday; "Israel's Private Arms Network" by Bishara A. Bahbah; "Arms Industries of the Middle East" by Joe Stork; "U.S. Military Contractors in Israel" by Sheila Ryan; "Turkey's Armaments Industries" by Ömer Karasapan; and "Low-Intensity Warfare: Key Strategy for the Third World Theatre" by Jochen Hippler.

A special feature in this issue of the magazine is a well-documented and well-illustrated "primer" on the militarization of the Middle East produced by the editors. The primer would be an excellent resource for educational programs about the Middle East and about U.S. military aid, weapons sales, and foreign intervention.

Hunter, Jane. *The Israeli-South African-U.S. Alliance.* Americans for Middle East Understanding. *The Link* 19, no. 1 (March-April 1986). 16pp. $2.50. Notes, photographs.

Israel has maintained its "normal" relationship with South Africa in spite of significant world opinion in favor of sanctions against the apartheid regime. This article explores that relationship: Israel as a trade partner and investor, as a conduit for military equipment, as a supplier of military advisors, as a mentor and cooperator in the development of nuclear weapons and devices—"South Africa having the uranium and Israel the technique." Israel has helped South Africa establish an up-to-date electronics industry. The two countries signed an agreement in 1985 to cooperate in the areas of science and technology.

The nearly unquestioned acceptance of Israel and Israeli policies in South Africa by the United States not only gives the Israel-South Africa relationship the nod of approval but also makes it difficult for the U.S. to act against apartheid.

Irani, George E. *The Vatican, U.S. Catholics and the Middle East.* Americans for Middle East Understanding. *The Link* 19, no. 3 (Aug.-Sept. 1986). 16pp. $2.50. Notes, photographs.

A public opinion survey in October 1982 on U.S. attitudes on the Middle East showed that 81 percent of American Catholics felt that Palestinians have the right to establish their own state on the West Bank and Gaza Strip. At the same time, 54 percent were against U.S. government recognition of the PLO and 63 percent were opposed to U.S. aid to Israel.

The Holy See and the U.S. Catholic hierarchy have definite positions in regard to the Middle East. This article explores the correspondence between the "official" positions and the positions expressed by the Catholic-in-the-street.

Topics covered include the Vatican and its relation to Judaism, Islam, the State of Israel, the Palestinians, Jerusalem, Middle East Catholics, and the conflict in Lebanon. A final section deals with policies of the U.S. Catholic church toward the Middle East as expressed in several documents written by U.S. bishops.

Jones, Allen K. *Iranian Refugees: The Many Faces of Persecution.* U.S. Committee for Refugees. *Issue Paper,* December 1984. 20pp. Free. References, photographs, maps, chronology.

The complicated situation in Iran following the overthrow of the Shah and the installation of the Ayatollah Ruhollah Khomeini is outlined in this concise summary. Brief details of the revolution, consolidation, and reconstruction as well as many other factors—the concept of an Islamic state, remnants of the Shah's supporters, revolutionary groups opposing the new regime—provide background to the understanding of the creation of refugee groups in Iran.

Ethnic and religious minorities, groups that have ideological differences with the ruling government, progressive, westernized Iranians, and women and children (recruited into the army as young as nine years of age) are those most likely to flee their country. Clearly, Iranian refugees are not a homogeneous group, not a group that can be easily categorized. This short study proceeds to examine the different ways in which Iranians have left their country and the different countries and situations in which they now find themselves. The numbers of Iranian refugees are in the hundreds of thousands, some say as many as one or two million. A final section in the pamphlet deals with the unique situation of Iranian refugees in the United States and recommends ways in which problems might be solved.

Joseph, Suad, et al. *Women and Politics in the Middle East.* **Middle East Research and Information Project.** *MERIP Middle East Report* **16, no. 1 (Jan.-Feb. 1986). 48pp. $3.50. Notes, interviews, photographs.**

The four major articles in this issue present an analysis of the nature of women's roles in the public sphere (state policy) and the domestic sphere (kin and community) that is unique in Middle East studies. In his introductory remarks Suad Joseph notes that "the discourse of public/domestic domains in the study of Middle East women has been relatively static, compared with feminist studies of other regions." By contrast, he says, the articles in *Women and Politics* "give accounts of fluid, shifting relationships. The boundaries are neither fixed nor irreversible. The state expands and retreats, kin and communal groups gain and lose control over members. Women's location and the definition of their activities shift as the boundaries move, or as they become more or less permeable."

Author Judith Tucker argues that as the Egyptian state developed, formal politics expanded and women's participation declined ("Insurrectionary Women: Women and the State in 19th Century Egypt"); Mary Hegland observes that the strengthening of the state in Iran under the Shah reduced local political factionalism and competition, an arena where women had been active ("Political Roles of Iranian Village Women"); Julie Peteet finds that among Palestinian women, politics has become an integral part of domesticity ("No Going Back: Women and the Palestinian Movement"); and Sondra Hale explains how the separation of public and domestic has been harmful to women in Sudan and argues that the reintegration of the two spheres would increase women's rights ("The Wing of the Patriarch: Sudanese Women and Revolutionary Parties").

Kapeliouk, Amnon. *Sabra and Shatila: Inquiry into a Massacre.* **Trans. and ed. Khalil Jahshan. Association of Arab-American University Graduates.** *Monograph,* **no. 19, 1983. 89pp. $5.95. Maps, photographs, notes.**

"Israel remains culpable," says Abdeen Jabara in his foreword, "for its failure to provide even a modicum of protection to the civilian population [in the Sabra and Shatila Palestinian refugee camps]." For this, and many other reasons, Jabara concludes that the Israeli government is criminally culpable for "direct and public incitement to commit genocide, complicity in genocide, or conspiracy to commit genocide."

Amnon Kapeliouk began the inquiry that led to Jabara's indictment the day after the shocking massacres at the Palestinian camps in West Beirut. It is based on testimony by dozens of Israelis (both civilian and military), Palestinians, Lebanese, and foreign journalists. "We have relied heavily on the Israeli, Lebanese, and international press," Kapeliouk states, "[as well as on] the depositions made before the Israeli judiciary commission of inquiry; the official proceedings of the Knesset (Israeli Parliament); the monitoring services of Middle East radio stations; the dispatches of international press agencies; and documents of Israeli, Palestinian, and Lebanese origin." The mass of evidence that Kapeliouk brings together in this pamphlet is overwhelming. As he notes, however, the Palestinians are unable to use any of this evidence to bring criminal charges against the Israeli government (for crimes against humanity) because they are a people without a formal nation-state.

The booklet closes with the author's comments on the official Israeli finding on the massacre.

Al-Khafaji, 'Isam, et al. *Wealth and Power in the Middle East.* Middle East Research and Information Project. *MERIP Middle East Report* 16, no. 5 (Sept.-Oct. 1986). 48pp. $3.50. Notes, photographs, statistical tables.

"Looking at wealth and power in the Middle East," write the editors of the *Middle East Report,* "we confront. . .images of ostentatious and undeserved wealth piled up by modern pirates — corrupt heads of state, venal merchants, and parasitic speculators and middlemen." The existence of this "entrepreneurial, production-oriented Middle Eastern bourgeoisie," the editors state, has been a well-kept secret.

Eight articles in this issue unveil the new economic and social power of the region's organized class of capitalists. The first two articles, by 'Isam al-Khafaji and Hanna Batatu, examine state and capitalism in Iraq. Subsequent articles treat Morocco's bourgeoisie, the exile bourgeoisie of Palestine, Turkey's super-rich, private capital in Israel, and Egypt's "infitah" bourgeoisie. Publisher Jim Paul contributes a survey article on the new bourgeoisie of the Gulf: Saudi Arabia, Kuwait, and the United Arab Emirates.

This issue is sprinkled with charts, personality profiles, and sidebar items that bring the holders of Middle Eastern wealth and power to life for the reader.

The editors acknowledge that many questions remain: How large is this class of capitalists? How fast is it growing? What are its cross-national links in the region and beyond? What is the relationship of the new bourgeoisie to political power, especially to the monarchies and the military who still dominate many of the countries in the region?

Khouri, Rami G. *For Those Who Share a Will to Live: Perspectives on a Just Peace in the Middle East.* Resource Center for Nonviolence. 1985. 38pp. $2.50.

This collection of essays was prepared to accompany the author's speaking tour in the United States in 1985. All but one of the essays was written for publication in the *Jordan Times*, for which Khouri served as editor-in-chief. One essay, "All the Children of Abraham," was written expressly for the U.S. tour.

Khouri's articles show his sensitivity to the Israeli peace movements as well as to the Arab situation. He criticizes U.S. policy toward the Palestinians and advocates a negotiated settlement that would guarantee the sovereign rights of both Israelis and Palestinians.

The essays treat several subjects: the reconciliation of Arab and Israeli claims to the land of Palestine, the relationship between the "separate sufferings" endured by Jews and Palestinians, the "intellectual terror of great powers who claim to oppose occupation while financing it," the scant results of the seventeenth session of the Palestine National Council, "terrorism," the Gulf war, the attacks on U.S. interests in the Middle East, and changes in the interpretation of the PLO national charter over the years.

Law, John. *Humphrey Goes to the Middle East.* Americans for Middle East Understanding. *The Link* 18, no. 5 (Dec. 1985). 16pp. $2.50. Illustration.

In 1982 John Law, author, editor, and journalist, first "met" Humphrey, "a well-meaning but aggressively obtuse and monumentally uninformed fellow." Humphrey has since then dropped by Law's office periodically to pick his brains on the Middle East. This visit takes place shortly after Humphrey has returned from a guided tour to Israel.

Law, student of and writer on the Middle East for almost forty years, and Humphrey, instant expert on the region, share their conversation with us. They cover topics ranging from a historical survey (starting from the beginnings of Zionism in 1905 and the growth of the idea of establishing a Jewish homeland in Palestine) to the question of who was there first and who were the foreign powers involved. The whole is a cleverly written and easy-to-read way to learn the bare bones about the Balfour Declaration, the Plan Dalet, Menachem Begin's terrorist group Irgun Zvai Leumi, the roles of Britain, Syria, the United States, and Egypt over the years, and the best-known "myths" surrounding the history of the region.

John Law was chief Middle East correspondent for *U.S. News and World Report* from 1953 to 1974.

***Lebanon's Revolt of the Dispossessed.* Middle East Research and Information Project. *MERIP Reports* 15, no. 5 (June 1985). 32pp. $2.75. Notes, interviews, photographs.**

MERIP editor Joe Stork opens this special issue on Lebanon with an exposition of the conflicting political forces within Lebanon. In the aftermath of the attacks on Palestinian camps in spring 1985 by Amal militia and Lebanese army troops Stork devotes a good deal of attention to the ten-year old armed movement known as Amal. He describes their origins and their agenda and assesses the strength of their challengers.

Salim Nasr, a researcher at CERMOC in Beirut, studies the roots of the Shi'i movement and describes its influence in Lebanon, while journalist Samir Kassir focuses his attention on the surprisingly powerful resistance forces in south Lebanon. Michael Gilsenan, author of "Recognizing Islam," offers very moving personal reflections on Lebanon at ground level. He describes his return to a war-wracked village that he had spent time in in the early 1970s.

A very useful "Lebanon Primer" and two interviews with U.S. relief workers with experience in Lebanon round out this issue.

Lebanon: Toward Legal Order and Respect for Human Rights. American Friends Service Committee. 1985. 2nd ed. 46pp. $2. Ten or more/ $1.50 each.

This forty-six-page report examines the Israeli occupation of Lebanon, the safety of civilians, the welfare of prisoners, and the degree of interference with Lebanese law and economy throughout the country.

McDowall, David. *The Kurds.* Minority Rights Group. *MRG Report,* no. 23, June 1985. New ed. 31pp. $3.95. Notes, photographs, maps, bibliography, appendix.

The vast majority of the world's sixteen million Kurdish people—the fourth most numerous people in the Middle East—live today confined to a mountainous region in the area where Turkey, Syria, Iran, and Iraq meet. The governments in the region—though divided on most political issues—are of one mind when it comes to the Kurds: these stateless people will not be given an independent nation of their own in that region. Who are the Kurds? What right do they have to claim a national identity? And what propects do they have for ever attaining such a goal?

The stated purpose of this MRG report is "to explore the identity of the Kurds, their bonds of loyalty and their historical and recent experience since the breakup of the Ottoman empire, to look at their position in the different countries in which they find themselves, and to pinpoint some of the factors and contradictions which exist today that both motivate and impede Kurdish nationalism."

Author McDowall describes the land, origins, religion, language, and societal formations of the Kurds and then gives a historical summary of the Kurdish people up to 1920. This is followed by a country-by-country treatment of the Kurds: in Turkey, Iran, Iraq, Syria, Lebanon, and the Soviet Union. This thorough MRG report closes with descriptions of the difficulties the Kurds have had in bringing their case before international bodies, such as the United Nations, and with a detailed summary of human rights abuses directed against the Kurdish people. McDowall warns that if all of the countries concerned—both the local powers and governments in Washington and Moscow—"fail to respond to Kurdish needs, then Kurdish statements of their existence and aspirations are likely to become more persistent and more extreme."

McDowall, David. *Lebanon: A Conflict of Minorities.* Minority Rights Group. *MRG Report,* no. 61, November 1983. 20pp. $4. Notes, documentation, tables, photographs, maps, bibliography, chronology.

The subtitle of this MRG report is indicative of the author's interpretation of the source of Lebanon's tortured history. "There can be few countries," McDowall writes, "which can claim to be so deeply and intrinsically composed of minorities as Lebanon — especially one so small that it could fit into one quarter of Switzerland. There is not a single resident in Lebanon," the author points out, "who cannot, in one sense or another, truthfully claim to belong to a minority."

Cognizant of this reality, McDowall aims in this booklet "to provide a background to the hopes, fears, and aspirations of [the minority] communities which have, all of them, already suffered too much. People in Lebanon have very long memories indeed," McDowall states, "and their outlook today can be considerably influenced by community experience — even centuries ago." *A Conflict of Minorities* dwells at length on the little-known history of this "community experience" and comes to the present and the future only in the last two pages of the booklet.

This report closes with a bibliography of twenty-eight books on or related to Lebanon.

Mutual Recognition between Israel and the Palestinians: The Path to Peace. **New Jewish Agenda. January 1987. 16pp. 25 cents. Bulk rates available. Map, action suggestions, illustrations, photographs, list of resources.**

This short pamphlet outlines the basic problem of one land–two peoples. Members of the group who produced the article see themselves as committed to the future of Israel, but also "believe that Israel cannot rule over Palestinians as an occupying force without undermining the Jewish and democratic ideals upon which the country was founded." They support "political and territorial compromise" on the part of both peoples.

The article suggests several options to deal with the conflict over the West Bank and the Gaza Strip, finally settling on one: a negotiated settlement "based upon the mutual recognition of each people's rights to self-determination; a renunciation of violence by both the Palestinians and the Israelis; Israeli withdrawal from the occupied territories; and creation of a sovereign Palestinian homeland." They reject any attempt at a military solution.

The present deadlock is examined as is the role of the United States and the Soviet Union and the threat to world peace. A "What You Can Do to Help" section suggests Educate, Lobby, Communicate, Dialogue, and Support.

The Palestinians in Israel and the Occupied Territories. **Institute for Palestine Studies.** *Journal of Palestine Studies* **14, no. 2 (Winter 1985). 305pp. $4.95. Notes, maps, statistical tables.**

This special issue of the *Journal* opens with a lengthy interview with Khalil al-Wazir, one of the founders of Fateh, after the closing of the seventeenth Palestine National Council in late November 1984. The articles that follow this interview are divided into two sections: (1) Palestinians in Israel, and (2) Palestinians in the Occupied Territories.

The first of the two sections contains articles on Israeli land seizures, Israeli control of the Bedouin, the future of Palestinian Arab education in Israel, and the political coming-of-age of the Arab "national minority" in Israel.

The second section opens with a fascinating series of interviews, "Voices from the Occupied Land," that aim "to represent the feelings and experiences of a cross-section of Palestinian society living under Israeli occupation." Two articles complete this section: "Palestinian Women Workers in the Israeli-Occupied Gaza Strip" by Susan Rockwell, and "Tug-of war: American Voluntary Organizations in the West Bank" by John P. Richardson.

Pieterse, Jan Nederveen. *Israel's Role in the Third World: Exporting West Bank Expertise.* **Emancipation Research. 1984. 36pp. $1.75. Notes, photographs.**

Israel is the fifth largest exporter of arms in the world and the largest supplier of arms to Latin America and Sub-Saharan Africa, according to estimates of the U.S. Central Intelligence Agency. But Israel's activities in Third World countries are "more wide ranging than just military sales," says author Jan Pieterse.

Pieterse describes Israel's role in detail and then searches for an understanding of how and why Israel is so heavily involved in Third World military affairs. He contends that the style of Israel's occupation of the West Bank and Gaza is, in fact, the "expertise" that Israel seeks to export to dictatorial regimes throughout the Third World. This "style" is a policy of exclusionism: we want the land, but we do not want the people.

The author situates this policy in the wider framework of Israel's relationship with the United States and of the political realities of the Middle East as a region.

Emancipation Research is a Netherlands-based foundation that focuses its work "on terrains neglected or inadequately presented in media or academic studies."

The PLO and Jordan. **Middle East Research and Information Project.** *MERIP Reports* **15, no. 3 (March-April 1985). 32pp. $2.75. Notes, photographs, documents, interview.**

This issue of *MERIP Reports* contains a major article by Naseer Aruri, professor of political science at Southeastern Massachusetts University, analyzing the role that Jordan can and should play in support of the Palestine Liberation Organization. Aruri reviews the history of Palestinian-Jordanian relations, focusing particularly on the period following the Israeli invasion of Lebanon in 1982. He analyzes, as well, Jordan's decision to restore diplomatic relations with Egypt and Syria's efforts "to dominate the Palestinian movement and to eliminate [Yasir] Arafat from the leadership."

A complementary article, "Hussein Hangover: The West Bank after the PNC," examines the accord announced on Feb. 11, 1985 between Jordan's King Hussein and PLO Chairman Yasir Arafat in the context of the contemporaneous 17th Palestine National Council held in Amman, Jordan.

Pratt, Cranford, et al. *Peace, Justice and Reconciliation in the Arab-Israeli Conflict: A Christian Perspective.* **Presbyterian Church (U.S.A.), General Assembly Mission Board. 1986. 64pp. Map.**

This booklet is a reprint of a publication issued by Friendship Press in 1979. The challenging insights offered by the seven Canadian authors of *Peace, Justice and Reconciliation* have stood well the test of time.

As Alan Geyer notes in his introduction to this booklet, "Canadian viewpoints on some topics have typically been in advance of both official policies and academic perspectives in ʹhe [United] States. . .and Canadian churches have often nurtured a prophetic vision of the things that make for peace" which deserved a much wider audience in the American churches."

For this reason the Presbyterian Church (U.S.A.) judged it appropriate to reissue this pamphlet and recommend it for use in a year-long church study program on the Middle East.

Throughout the academic year 1977–78 the seven authors of this study grappled with "what might be the main components of a responsible Christian position regarding the Middle East." Each of the authors had had "some interest over the years in issues related to Israel," but they all acknowledged the need for "a redefinition of our priorities as Christians and as North Americans." This "position paper" is the result of their joint efforts to understand the history and current realities of the Middle East and to fashion a "moral perspective" on the Arab-Israeli conflict.

Roberts, Adam, Boel Joergensen, and Frank Newman. *Academic Freedom under Israeli Military Occupation.* **World University Service. 87pp. $2. Available from the American Friends Service Committee.**

This report for the World University Service is an inquiry into the state of higher education in the West Bank and Gaza under the Israeli military authorities. The authors describe the history of the region and analyze the impact of Israeli occupation on six educational institutions.

Rokach, Livia. *Israel's Sacred Terrorism: A Study of Moshe Sharett's "Personal Diary."* **Association of Arab-American University Graduates. *Information Paper,* no. 23, 1985. 3rd ed. 90pp. $5.95. Notes, appendixes.**

Moshe Sharett, Israel's first foreign minister and prime minister from 1953 to 1955, kept a personal diary that is the subject of this pamphlet. *Israel's Sacred Terrorism* uses Sharett's own words to illustrate how Israel's "security establishment," men like David Ben Gurion, Arik Sharon, and Moshe Dayan, sought to destabilize neighboring Arab countries through covert military operations and terrorist activity, and plotted the takeover of south Lebanon, the West Bank, and Gaza.

"Livia Rokach has performed a valuable service," writes Noam Chomsky in his foreword, "in making this material readily available, for the first time, to those who are interested in discovering the real world that lies behind 'official history.'"

Rubenberg, Cheryl. *The Misguided Alliance.* Americans for Middle East Understanding. *The Link* 19, no. 4 (Oct.-Nov. 1986). 16pp. $2.50. Notes, photographs.

Is Israel an asset or a liability to the United States? This historical survey of the Israel-United States relationship speaks to this question. First the article examines the most common arguments supporting the claim that Israel is a "strategic asset" for the United States: a check for Soviet expansionism in the Middle East, a military force to maintain regional stability, a safeguard against domestic insurrection in pro-American Arab countries, a source of intelligence information, a promoter of U.S. corporate and commercial interests, and a democracy amongst non-democracies in the Middle East.

The second part of the article traces the history of the "strategic asset" thesis from the time of the Truman Administration on to the Reagan Administration.

Dr. Cheryl A. Rubenberg is the author of *Israel and the American National Interest* (University of Illinois Press).

Rubenberg, Cheryl. *The Palestine Liberation Organization: Its Institutional Infrastructure.* Institute of Arab Studies. *IAS Monograph Series,* no. 1, 1983. 66pp. $4.95. Available from the Association of Arab-American University Graduates.

This pamphlet is a study of the civilian institutions and services through which the Palestine Liberation Organization serves the needs of hundreds of thousands of Palestinians in the areas of health, education, and welfare. The IAS monograph presents information on a little-known aspect of the PLO's international work and one that represents a unique experiment in the functioning of a national liberation movement.

Ryan, Sheila, and Muhammad Hallaj. *Palestine Is, but Not in Jordan.* Association of Arab-American University Graduates. *Information Paper,* no. 24, 1983. 36pp. $3.50. Maps, notes.

This booklet effectively challenges the myth that there is already a homeland for the Palestinians, and that it is Jordan. "By selective historical abstractions and creative technique," writes Faith Zeadey for AAUG, "this claim [i.e., that Palestine is Jordan], manufactured by Israeli officials, not only denies the Palestinian his homeland, but denies the basis of his just struggle." "Such flagrant deception," Zeadey concludes, "serves only to promote the injustices and to ensure the failure of any attempt at a just settlement of the Palestinian issue and the wider issues of the Middle East conflict."

Sadowski, Yahya M. *Asad's Syria.* Middle East Research and Information Project. *MERIP Reports* 15, no. 6 (July-Aug. 1985). 32pp. $2.75. Notes, interview, illustrations, tables, photographs, maps.

This issue of *MERIP Reports* focuses on the Syria of Hafiz al-Asad. It contains three lengthy articles: "Cadres, Guns and Money: The Eighth Regional Congress of the Syrian Ba'th" by Yahya M. Sadowski, a political science professor at the University of California, Berkeley;

"Syria in Lebanon" by William Harris, a scholar who is researching Syrian and Israeli perspectives towards Lebanon; and "The Syrian Working Class Today" by Elisabeth Longuenesse, who has worked with the French Institute for Arab Studies in Damascus and the Center for Studies and Research on the Contemporary Middle East in Beirut.

Also included in this issue are excerpts from interviews with two Palestinian activists in Damascus concerning the contentious truce that was signed after the assault on the Palestinian camps in Beirut.

Shakrah, Jan Abu. *The Making of a Non-Person*. Americans for Middle East Understanding. *The Link* 19, no. 2 (May-June 1986). 16pp. $2.50. Notes, photographs.

Sociologist Jan Abu Shakrah examines the process of dehumanization and depersonalization in the Israeli-Palestinian context. At first glance the study seems to simply analyze the dehumanization of the Palestinian people; it is really a study of what has happened to both Israelis and Palestinians in the course of their conflict, since "the attempt to dehumanize the other corrupts the dehumanizer" as well.

Drawing on the insights of Martin Buber, Victor Frankl, Frantz Fanon, Paulo Freire, and Carl Rogers, Abu Shakrah traces in step-by-step fashion the "making of a non-person": taking the person from the land, torture and *tertur* (the systematic harassment and humiliation of the occupied populace by army troops and border police), and futurelessness. Finally, Jan Abu Shakrah considers the future—"Hoping against Hope"—and makes the plea for "genuine dialogue" between Israelis and Palestinians.

The author is an American who lives with her Palestinian husband and two sons in "the heart of this conflict."

Steele, Jonathan, et al. *Hidden Wars*. Middle East Research and Information Project. *MERIP Middle East Report* 16, no. 4 (July-Aug. 1986). 48pp. $3.50. Notes, tables, maps.

Hidden Wars contains in-depth reports on three heavily militarized areas: Afghanistan, Kurdistan, and Pakistan.

Jonathan Steele, chief foreign correspondent for *The Guardian* (London), contributes the opening article on Afghanistan: "Moscow's Kabul Campaign." Martin van Bruinessen, author of *Agha, Shaikh and State: On the Social and Political Organization of Kurdistan,* writes about "The Kurds between Iran and Iraq." Journalist Jamal Rashid reports from Pakistan on "Pakistan and the Central Command."

Stevens, Janet. *Israeli Use of U.S. Weapons in Lebanon*. Association of Arab-American University Graduates. *Information Papers*, no. 25, 1983. 62pp. $3.50. Photographs, appendixes.

This report contains firsthand accounts of the human suffering and property damage caused by Israel's use of U.S. weapons during its 1982 invasion of Lebanon.

Stevens divides her study into two parts: (1) Israel's use of U.S.-supplied military equipment in Lebanon, and (2) Israel's war on Lebanon's civilian population. The entire second half of the pamphlet (the appendixes) contains numerous Congressional reports and newspaper articles substantiating Stevens's findings.

Stork, Joe, et al. *The Future of the Gulf.* Middle East Research and Information Project. *MERIP Reports* 15, no. 4 (May 1985). 32pp. $2.75. Notes, interviews, tables, photographs, maps.

"All of the small Arab states of the Persian Gulf are now well into their second decade as independent political entities," writes MERIP editor Joe Stork in the opening article in this issue. How have these states fared with their independence? And how well will the ruling classes of the Gulf weather the war and revolution that swirl throughout the Gulf region? Stork's article, "Prospects for the Gulf," addresses these vital questions.

Rob Franklin and 'Abd ul-Hadi Khalaf, a Bahraini sociologist now living in Cyprus, each contribute articles on Bahrain: "Migrant Labor and the Politics of Development in Bahrain" (Franklin) and "Labor Movements in Bahrain" (Khalaf). Eric Rouleau, the chief foreign correspondent for *Le Monde,* writes about the Palestinian diaspora in the Gulf and Smith College professor of politics Fred Lawson offers a detailed analysis of "class and state" in Kuwait.

This issue also includes an interview ("The Rulers Are Afraid of Their Own People") with an anonymous Bahraini citizen and a page-length review of Fuad Khuri's *Tribe and State in Bahrain* (University of Chicago, 1980) by "a Bahrain correspondent."

Stork, Joe, et al. *Nuclear Shadow over the Middle East.* Middle East Research and Information Project. *MERIP Middle East Report* 16, no. 6 (Nov.-Dec. 1986). 48pp. $3.50. Notes, figures, tables, photographs, maps.

MERIP editor Joe Stork contributed two of the nuclear-related articles in this issue of the *Middle East Report*: the introductory overview, "Nuclear Shadow over the Middle East," and "Pakistan's Nuclear Fix." Assistant editor Martha Wenger surveys the evidence that points to Israel's possession of nuclear weapons and Jane Hunter, editor and publisher of *Israeli Foreign Affairs,* presents startling revelations about Israel's cooperation with South Africa in the production of nuclear weapons.

Less than one half of this issue is actually devoted to a discussion of the "nuclear shadow over the Middle East," but the articles are so unique and so well done that the issue is highly recommended, especially to anti-nuclear educators and activists. U.S. taxpayers should also be interested in how their tax dollars are being used to further the nuclear ambitions of two of the countries treated in this issue, Israel and Pakistan.

Stork, Joe, et al. *The Struggle for Food.* Middle East Research and Information Project. *MERIP Middle East Report* 17, no. 2 (March-April 1987). 48pp. $3.50. Notes, figures, photographs, maps, recommended readings, statistical tables.

This issue of the *Report* contains eight substantial articles and complementary sidebar materials on a variety of food-related issues in the Middle East.

Joe Stork and Karen Pfeifer provide the overview article, "Bullets, Banks and Bushels: The Struggle for Food in the Middle East." Vahid Nowshirvani, of Columbia University's Middle East Institute, contributes "The Yellow Brick Road: Self-Sufficiency or Self-Enrichment in Saudi Agriculture?" Cornell University's Douglas Gritzinger assesses the prospects for greater irrigation of the Middle East's arid lands, "New Lands Irrigation: Promise or Panacea?" Robert Springborg's discussion of Iraq's efforts to back away from public control of agrarian production appeared in longer form in the winter 1986 issue of the *Middle East Journal.*

In "The Language of Food: PL 480 in Egypt" Jean-Jacques Dethier and Kathy Funk describe the policies — including the U.S. government's PL 480 food aid program — that have turned Egypt from being a leading granary for the entire Mediterranean into one of the largest markets for U.S. agricultural exports. Ethiopia and the Horn of Africa are the subject of articles by two international relief workers. Dan Connell, executive director of Grassroots International, writes about the Horn of Africa as "the scene of one of the most spectacular geopolitical realignments in Cold War history" ("Alignments in the Horn: Famine Reshuffles the Deck") and Gayle Smith looks at the politics of famine relief in Ethiopia.

In the final article in this issue — a reprint from *African Business* — Steve Askin analyzes the way in which top officials of the Somali government diverted U.S. food aid "from the most needy to enrich their friends and to feed the army fighting a long-running border war with Ethiopia."

Tabari, Azar. *The Rise of Islam: What Did Happen to Women?* *Khamsin,* **1983. 10pp. $1.50. Available from Women's International Resource Exchange Service.**

This brief article from the socialist journal, *Khamsin,* examines the historical impact of Islam on women, including the effects of changes in interpretation of Islamic law in terms of marriage, divorce, chastity, and property rights. Tabari's article is particularly relevant in view of the current Iranian government's use of "Islamic" law to return women to the household and the veil. The author, an Iranian scholar in exile, concludes that historically women have experienced periods of relative liberation in Islamic countries, but invariably, as Islam becomes the state religion, the oppression of women becomes institutionalized.

Tarbush, Mohammad. *Reflections of a Palestinian.* **American-Arab Affairs Council. 1986. 96pp. $5.95.**

Mohammad Tarbush's short, personal articles and letters in this booklet chronicle in simple and readable style his geographical and political journey through times of turmoil.

"Israel came into existence by the negation of the Palestinians and their right to nationhood," the author states. He proposes that the European media have treated the Palestinian position more fairly and responsively than have the North American media. Frederick Axelyard echoes the author's sentiments in his introduction: "Palestinian nationalism is poised to fall through the cracks in a world system that is apparently eager to hasten its disappearance. It would be more convenient for the rest of the world if the Palestinians simply accepted the status quo."

Time Is Running Out. **American Friends Service Committee. 1983. 8pp. 20 cents. 100/$15.**

This AFSC pamphlet addresses the significance of the Israeli settlement on the West Bank and the continued expansion that is an obstacle to the development of peace negotiations — negotiations that would lead to mutual recognition, self-determination, and security for Israelis and Palestinians.

Turkey and the Middle East. **American Academic Association for Peace in the Middle East.** *Middle East Review* **17, no. 3 (Spring 1985). 60pp. $4. Notes, maps.**

The centuries-long rule of the Ottoman empire, precursor of today's Turkish Republic, over the Arab world ended only seventy years ago. Yet today Turkey, still an important nation of that region, is scarcely mentioned in the newspapers and is little known by Americans. This issue of the *Middle East Review* examines modern Turkey, showing aspects of "a country which is, in a variety of ways, a key to the understanding of central elements of internal conflict and development in the Muslim world as a whole, as well as in the Middle East in particular."

Articles explore recent developments in Turkey's political and economic life, showing changing relations with Israel, as well as with Arab and other Muslim states. Turkey's turn to secularism and the ambivalence toward Islam of its intellectuals and leaders, a result of its revolution, is of some interest. Turkey once had the duty, as seat of the Islamic caliphate, of "representing and defending Islamic rights and claims everywhere." Now its separation of religion and state gives Turkey a special position in a region where the two are practically inseparable. It is the only Muslim state (except Egypt), for example, to maintain diplomatic relations with Israel. Turkey is not completely divorced from the Islamic world, however. It seems not to find itself completely at home in either the Western world (from whence its arms and aid come) or the Islamic world.

The articles are somewhat scholarly but quite readable. They are certainly informative about this usually ignored country of the Middle East.

Wake, Jim, Deena Hurwitz, and **R. Scott Kennedy, eds.** *Looking at the Middle East Puzzle.* **Humanitas International Human Rights Committee and the Resource Center for Nonviolence. 1983. 36pp. $1. Graph, illustrations, photographs, maps, notes, list of resources.**

The editors of this attractive pamphlet present "several perspectives which [they] hope will contribute to a better understanding of the issues that surround the [Arab/Israeli] conflict." The articles are addressed primarily to North Americans and are intended to help inform them of "the possibilities and proponents" of peace in the Middle East. The editors encourage the readers to proceed with an open mind and to move on to actively promote "constructive dialogue."

Jim Wake writes of his first trip to the Middle East as part of a seventeen-member "peace-study delegation." In another article he reports (with Deena Hurwitz) on Israeli settlements in the occupied territories (West Bank, Gaza Strip, Golan Heights). R. Scott Kennedy, whose most recent trip to the Middle East was his tenth, writes on the PLO — a most instructive article considering the one-dimensional image most of us have of that organization. In another article, Kennedy tells the story of the 13,000 Druze (Syrians) who remained in their villages in the Golan Heights after the 1967 Arab/Israeli War resisting nonviolently the offer of Israeli citizenship. Judy Blanc, a member of the steering committee of the Committee Against the War in Lebanon and of the Israleft collective, describes the Israeli Peace Movement. Nat Hentoff's article on the silence of most American Jews first appeared in *The Village Voice*. Seth Tillman's article, a chapter from his book *The United States in the Middle East*, explores ways in which the United States might contribute to a Middle East peace.

In line with their desire to inspire the reader to act, the editors include a page of resources, citing materials for further study and organizations to contact for ongoing actions.

Wingerter, Rex B. *The Palestine-Israel Conflict in the U.S. Courtroom.* **Americans for Middle East Understanding.** *The Link* **18, no. 3 (Sept. 1985). 16pp. $2.50. Notes, illustrations, photographs.**

The "special relationship" between the United States and Israel is here scrutinized as it has found expression in the U.S. courts. Lawyer and Middle East specialist Rex Wingerter describes six cases. These cases are significant, says Wingerter, because the decisions made set precedent. In our system of jurisprudence, precedents set in regard to any Constitutional right go far beyond the particular case to eventually affect all citizens.

One case, for example, involved the extradition of a young Palestinian from a Chicago prison to Israel. Before this case U.S. courts had abided by the "political offense exception" doctrine of extradition law. Now it is "irreparably altered."

In another case, a lawyer, Abdeen Jabara, a second-generation American of Lebanese origin, who lectured and wrote against U.S. policy toward the Middle East and who supported the Palestinians' struggle, was under surveillance for seven years — even after the U.S. government had concluded that he was innocent of any criminal activity. Jabara brought suit against the FBI. The lower courts decided against Jabara and the U.S. Supreme Court refused to review his appeal. Such decisions considerably weaken the force of the Fourth Amendment protecting any citizen from warrantless searches and seizures.

Each case described by Wingerter is unique; altogether the study is sobering.

Wright, Claudia. *The Politics of Liquidation: The Reagan Adminis-tration Policy toward the Arabs.* **Association of Arab-American University Graduates.** *Occasional Paper,* **no. 10, 1986. 8pp. $1.50. Notes.**

In this booklet, author Claudia Wright claims that the Reagan Administration has pursued a policy of liquidation toward Libya's Mu'ammar Qadhafi since 1981, a policy that violates international law and constitutes only one element of an overall design to establish Israel as Washington's "policeman" over Arab peoples and governments.

Responding to Wright's charges, University of Illinois (Champaign) professor of law Francis A. Boyle warns that "if the American people do not act in opposition to this policy now, then Wright's prediction, that the international legal right of the Palestinian people to self-determination will be extinguished next, can only come true."

Wright, Claudia. *Spy, Steal and Smuggle: Israel's Special Relation-ship with the United States.* **Association of Arab-American University Graduates.** *Special Report,* **no. 5, 1986. 33pp. $4.50. Notes.**

Israel argues that, as a strategic ally already privy to highly sensitive U.S. government information, its espionage and other subversive activities against the United States do not threaten U.S. security. Claudia Wright shows why this alibi for violating U.S. law should be rejected. In *Spy, Steal and Smuggle* she details how the Israelis, operating both clandestinely and overtly, present a dangerous threat to the national security and the economic security of the United States by penetrating the U.S. government, its intelligence agencies, and U.S. defense industries.

SUPPLEMENTARY LIST OF PAMPHLETS AND ARTICLES

MIDDLE EAST GENERAL

Alnasrawi, Abbas. *Arab Oil and U.S. Energy Requirements.* Association of Arab-American University Graduates. *Monograph,* no. 16, 1982. 88pp. $5.95.

Halliday, Fred, et al. *Migrant Workers in the Middle East*. Middle East Research and Information Project. *MERIP Reports* 14, no. 4 (May 1984). 32pp. $2.75.

Holland, Max. *The Militarization of the Middle East*. American Friends Service Committee. 1983. $1. 30pp. Ten or more/75 cents each.

Klare, Michael. *The Deadly Connection*. Middle East Research and Information Project. *MERIP Reports* 14, no. 9 (Nov.-Dec. 1984). 32pp. $2.75.

Abu-Lughod, Ibrahim, ed. *The Islamic Alternative*. Association of Arab-American University Graduates and Institute for Arab Studies. *Arab Studies Quarterly* 4, nos. 1–2 (Spring 1982). $10.

Middle East Project, Fellowship of Reconciliation, and War Resisters League. *The Middle East Arms/Nuke Connection*. American Friends Service Committee. 1982. 8pp. 25 cents. 5/$1, 25/$3.

Statements and Position Papers of Major American Organizations on Middle East Peace. Washington Middle East Associates. 1985. $4.

Taylor, Elizabeth, et al. *Women and Labor Migration*. Middle East Research and Information Project. *MERIP Reports* 14, no. 5 (June 1984). 32pp. $2.75.

Viorst, Milton. *UNRWA and Peace in the Middle East*. Middle East Institute. *Special Study,* no. 4, 1984. 62pp. $3.95.

Zeadey, Faith, ed. *Camp David: A New Balfour Declaration*. Association of Arab-American University Graduates. *Special Report,* no. 3, 1979. 90pp. $4.75.

ARABIAN PENINSULA AND THE GULF

Hiro, Dilip, et al. *The Strange War in the Gulf.* Middle East Research and Information Project. *MERIP Reports* 14, nos. 6–7 (July-Sept. 1984). 64pp. $4.50.

Molyneux, Maxine. *Socialist Revolution and Women's Rights in Democratic Yemen*. Women's International Resource Exchange Service. 12pp. 90 cents.

Owen, Dr. Roger. *Migrant Workers in the Gulf.* Minority Rights Group. *MRG Report,* no. 68, 1985. 24pp. $3.95.

FERTILE CRESCENT

Committee on the Exercise of the Inalienable Rights of the Palestinian People, United Nations. *The International Status of the Palestinian People*. United Nations. 1981. 32pp.

Ennes, James M., Jr. *The USS Liberty Affair*. Americans for Middle East Understanding. *The Link* 17, no.2 (May-June 1984). 16pp. $3.50.

Feldman, Avigdor. *The West Bank: Oppression by Law.* Palestine Research and Educational Center. *Life under Occupation Series,* no. 2, Jan. 1984. Free.

Focus: Israel. Shmate, no. 9, Summer 1984. 28pp. $4.

Fosse, Erik, Ebba Wergeland, and Ibrahim Abu-Lughod, eds. *Israel and the Question of Palestine.* Association of Arab-American University Graduates and Institute for Arab Studies. *Arab Studies Quarterly* 7, nos. 2–3 (Spring/Summer 1985). $10.

Hallaj, Muhammad. *Palestine: The Suppression of an Idea.* Association of Arab-American University Graduates. *Occasional Paper,* no. 8, 1983. 40pp. $2.

Hallaj, Muhammad. *The Palestinians and the PLO.* Palestine Research and Educational Center. *Information Papers Series,* no. 1, September 1983. 12pp. $1.

The Iron Fist: Israel's Occupation of South Lebanon, 1982-1985. American-Arab Anti-Discrimination Committee. *Issue Paper,* no. 17, 1985.

Lebanon and Palestine 1982. Association of Arab-American University Graduates and Institute for Arab Studies. *Arab Studies Quarterly* 4, no. 4 (Fall 1982). $5.

McDowall, David. *The Palestinians.* Minority Rights Group. *MRG Report,* no. 24, 1986. Rev. ed. 19pp. $3.95.

Moleah, Alfred T. *Israel and South Africa: Partners in Repression.* Palestine Research and Educational Center. *Information Papers Series,* no. 2, January 1984. $1.

Nakhleh, Khalil. *The Two Galilees.* Association of Arab-American University Graduates. *Occasional Paper,* no. 7, 1982. 27pp. $1.50.

Nevo, Naomi, and David Solomonica. *Ideological Change of Rural Women's Role and Status: A Case Study of Family Based Cooperative Villages in Israel.* Women in International Development, Michigan State University. *Working Papers on Women in International Development,* no. 16, 1983. 21pp. $2.75.

Playfair, Emma. *Administrative Detention in the Occupied West Bank.* Al-Haq/Law in the Service of Man. *Occasional Paper,* no. 1, 1986. 54pp. $5.

A Plea for the Innocent. American Friends Service Committee. 1983. 8pp. 25 cents. 100/$10.

Questions and Answers about the Arab-Israeli-Palestinian Conflict. American Friends Service Committee. 1983. 8pp. 25 cents. 100/$15.

Questions and Answers on Lebanon. American Friends Service Committee. 1983. 28pp. $1. Ten or more/75 cents each.

Rishmawi, Mona. *Planning in Whose Interest? Land Use Planning as a Strategy for Judaization.* Al-Haq/Law in the Service of Man. *Occasional Paper,* no. 4, Dec. 1986. 20pp.

Shahak, Israel. *Israel's Global Role: Weapons for Repression.* Association of Arab-American University Graduates. *Special Report,* no. 4, 1982. 61pp. $3.75. Introduction by Noam Chomsky.

Sobol, Yehoshua. *You Can Only Weep.* Palestine Research and Educational Center. *Life under Occupation Series,* no. 1, September 1983. Free.

U.S. Assistance to the State of Israel: The Uncensored Draft Report. American-Arab Anti-Discrimination Committee. 1983. 78pp. $4.50.

Ziadeh, Susan, and Elaine Hagopian, eds. *Realignment of Power in Lebanon: Internal and External Dimensions.* Association of Arab-American University Graduates and Institute for Arab Studies. *Arab Studies Quarterly* 7, no. 4 (Fall 1985). $5.

NORTH AFRICA

Fortney, Judith A., et al. *Causes of Death to Women of Reproductive Age in Egypt.* Women in International Development, Michigan State University. *Working Papers on Women in International Development,* no. 49, 1984. 15pp. $2.50.

Morsy, Soheir A. *Familial Adaptations to the Internationalization of Egyptian Labour.* Women in International Development, Michigan State University. *Working Papers on Women in International Development,* no. 94, 1985. 28pp. $2.75.

Paul, Jim, et al. *Insurrection in North Africa.* Middle East Research and Information Project. *MERIP Reports* 14, no. 8 (Oct. 1984). 32pp. $2.75.

Scobie, Grant M. *Food Subsidies and the Government Budget in Egypt.* International Food Policy Research Institute. *Working Papers on Food Subsidies,* no. 2, November 1985. 40pp. Free.

IRAN

Mahdi, Ali-Akbar. *Women, Religion, and the State: Legal Developments in Twentieth Century Iran.* Women in International Development, Michigan State University. *Working Papers on Women in International Development,* no. 38, 1983. 14pp. $2.25.

TURKEY

Ahmad, Feroz. *Turkey under Military Rule.* Middle East Research and Information Project. *MERIP Reports* 14, no. 3 (March-April 1984). 32pp. $2.75.

Barchard, David. *State Terror in Turkey.* Middle East Research and Information Project. *MERIP Reports* 14, no. 2 (Feb. 1984). 32pp. $2.75.

INFORMATION SOURCES

Back issues of several of the periodicals that appear in this chapter make excellent resource materials for group or individual study. We especially recommend *The Link* from Americans for Middle East Understanding, and MERIP's *Middle East Report*. See, as well, the entire series of monographs, occasional papers, and reports from the Association of Arab-American University Graduates (AAUG).

AAUG, Al-Haq/Law in the Service of Man, the American Friends Service Committee, Minority Rights Group, and many of the other organizations listed in this chapter, all publish catalogs of pamphlets and other low-priced resource materials.

Perhaps the most comprehensive source of information about articles on the Middle East — though not necessarily in reprinted form — is the Middle East Institute's quarterly *Middle East Journal*. Each issue contains a lengthy listing of annotated articles, from a variety of magazines, arranged by subject.

For a compendium of these articles, see *Articles on the Middle East, 1947-1971: A Cumulation of the Bibliographies* from *The Middle East Journal*. Comp. Peter M. Rossi, Wayne E. White, and Arthur E. Goldschmidt, Jr. Ann Arbor, Mich.: Pierian Press, 1980. 4 vols. 1,646pp.

See also the publications from **Third World Resources**, described in the preface to this resource directory.

I sit in administrative detention
The reason, sir, is that I am an Arab.
An Arab who refused to sell his soul
Who had always striven, sir, for freedom.
An Arab who has protested the suffering of his people
Who has carried with him the hope of a just peace,
Who has spoken out against death in every corner
Who has called for — and has lived — a fraternal life.
That is why I sit in administrative detention
Because I carried on the struggle
And because I am an Arab.

Fawzi El Asmar

Audiovisuals

This chapter is divided into two parts: visual resources (films, filmstrips, slideshows, and videotapes) and audio resources (records and tapes). The part entitled **visual resources** is divided into three sections: annotated entries, supplementary list, and sources of additional information. The part devoted to **audio resources** has two subdivisions: annotated entries and sources of additional information.

It was impossible for us to preview all the audiovisuals included in this directory. In the case of resources that we were unable to evaluate personally, we have quoted directly from the distributor's description of the audiovisual or from annotations in other directories. The source is given in small capital letters at the end of each annotation: DIST / distributor. Remarks that are not within quotation marks are those of the editors.

We have done our best to select audiovisuals that appear to be worthy of your consideration, but we caution you to arrange for previews of audiovisuals to determine their appropriateness in your setting.

All audiovisuals are integrated into the titles index at the back of this directory. See the organizations index for the addresses of distributors listed in this chapter.

(See p. 115 for the introduction to the audio resources part of this chapter.)

VISUAL RESOURCES

Information in the **annotated entries** is given in the following order: title; producer(s); director(s); date; length (in minutes); format; principal rental and purchase price; secondary distributor(s); description of content; and source of annotation.

When an audiovisual is available from distributors other than the principal one, we have listed those as secondary distributors, but in deference to the rights of the principal distributor we have omitted the often lower rental rates of the secondary distributors. You are free, of course, to make your own inquiries. Rental/purchase information should be taken only as being indicative. We urge you to inquire about all fees and conditions before ordering an audiovisual. Some distributors have sliding price scales depending upon the nature of your organization and the intended use of the audiovisual, so it is advisable to ask about discounts when you make your inquiry.

Visual resources in the **supplementary list** (pp. 110–114) are grouped under these headings: Middle East general; Arabian Peninsula and Gulf; Fertile Crescent; North Africa; and Islam.

The **information sources** section (pp. 114–115) provides information on guides and catalogs that contain the names of other visual resources related to the Middle East.

ANNOTATED ENTRIES

The Arab and the Israeli. **Produced by Public Broadcasting System. 1984. Videocassette. Distributor: American Friends Service Committee (Cambridge). Rental: $15. Also from EcuFilm ($20).**

"The story of the historic 1984 U.S. joint tour of an Israeli (Mordechai Bar-on, former high-level Israeli official) and a Palestinian (Mohammed Milhem, former Palestinian mayor in the occupied West Bank). They discuss peace for the Middle East and a resolution of the Israeli-Palestinian conflict. Aired by the Frontline program on PBS. The tour was arranged by AFSC and New Jewish Agenda." DIST

The Arab Experience. **Color filmstrip with cassette tape. 5 parts, teacher's guide, and library kit. Distributor: Guidance Associates. Purchase: $197. Also available in filmstrips-on-video format. Order no. 06092–860.**

"This program takes students into different Arab societies within the Middle East, where modernism and tradition coexist. It examines the social impact of continuing conflict in the region and the effect of wealth on oil-producing Arab nations and on the world. On-location photography and interviews create a detailed portrait of Arab life today. The program explores the rise of Islam, the Arab-Zionist conflict, the Palestinian refugee problem, and the Arab nationalism of Nasser and other leaders." DIST

The Arabs Now. **Written by Basim Musallam. Directed by Colin Luke. 50 minutes. Color film and videocassette. With study guide. Major locations: Cairo, Lebanon, the Arabian Gulf, and Morocco. The Arabs: A Living History Series. Distributor: Landmark Films. Purchase: $495.**

"What do the Arabs believe to be the most potent forces in their society at the present time and how do they assess their condition today?

"How possible is criticism of that condition and who will be the most effective critics? The intellectuals? The politicians? Arab youth? Fifty percent of all Arabs are under the age of twenty and twenty million

Arab children are in school today. What effect will this explosion in education have on society? What will be the effect of the huge labor migrations across the Arab world or the revolution in communications, as air travel, television, video, and satellites serve to bring Arabs of all nations into close contact with one another?

"Just how successful have the Arab political orders been in coping with all the needs and pressures of our time and what future developments are likely or possible?

"Writer Basim Musallam returns to the Arab world for this final program in the Living History Series, to ask the questions that Arabs ask themselves; not in the hope of finding definitive answers, for those are beyond reach, but in order to allow the Western viewer to share in those concerns which are uppermost in the Arabs' own minds." DIST

Beirut: On a Clear Day You Can See Peace. **Produced by Grassroots International and Women for Peace in Lebanon. 1984. 30 minutes. Color videocassette. Distributor: Third World Newsreel. Purchase: $200. Rental: $50.**

"Focusing primarily on the women of Beirut, this video shows the heartbreaking plight of families with no homes, no electricity, little food, and less hope. Once regarded as the "jewel of the Mediterranean," an international banking center, and tourist attraction, Beirut has become a battlefield with thirty percent of the population Palestinian refugees.

"In 1982, Israel invaded Lebanon to squash the alliances being formed between Palestinians and Lebanese struggling against Phalangist control. This video goes behind the headlines and television clips of bombed-out buildings to show us the people who must live in the devastation of war-torn Beirut. Interviews are conducted in the midst of shelling attacks. A man tells of how his wife and eight children were murdered before his eyes during the Shatila massacre. In a shelter, a very old woman with useless legs sobs to the filmmaker that she has no one left, even as a baby is being born right next to her. Another woman berates the filmmakers: 'Instead of photographing, go bring back the missing ones.'" DIST

Between Two Worlds. **Written by Abdallah Hammoudi. Directed by Colin Luke. 1986. 50 minutes. Color film and videocassette. With study guide. Location: Fez, Morocco. The Arabs: A Living History Series. Distributor: Landmark Films. Purchase: $495.**

"What was Arab society like during the thousand-year period following the decline of the Arab Empire? What memories, what feelings, does it provoke in the minds of today's Arabs, caught as they are in the turbulence of twentieth century change?

"Abdelmalek Tazi is a member of an influential family of Fez — ancient seat of the rulers of Morocco. As Abdelmalek plays with his children, looks for business contacts in the Arabian Gulf states, prays at his father's tomb, or revisits his childhood haunts in the medieval quarter of Fez, our writer, Abdallah Hammoudi, questions how deeply the manners, beliefs, attitudes, and values of the old Arab world penetrate the lives of modern Arabs. As he says: 'Is it really possible to be an Arab in that traditional world and in the world of tomorrow?'" DIST

Blood and Sand: War in the Sahara. **Produced by Sharon Sopher. 1982. 56 minutes. Color film and videocassette. Distributor: First Run Features. Rental: $100 (film only). Purchase: $950 (film), $500 (video).**

"*Blood and Sand* is the first film to report on America's involvement in the Western Sahara war. Through careful research and documentation, the film examines the conflict between the Polisario guerrillas, native people of the Western Sahara fighting for the liberation of their land, and the Kingdom of Morocco which now occupies the territory.

"Emmy-award winning producer Sharon Sopher traveled hundreds of miles of barren desert on both sides of the battlefront to record the emotions, thinking, and lifestyle of the people fighting this war. In addition, the film presents interviews with key policymakers in the Carter and Reagan administrations, including former National Security Advisor Zbigniew Brzezinski.

"*Blood and Sand* offers a detailed account of how U.S. involvement has escalated the war through arms sales and is a powerful and critical analysis of American foreign policy." DIST

Building a Nation. **Written by Mahfoud Bennoune. Directed by Colin Luke. 1986. 50 minutes. Color film and videocassette. With study guide. Location: Algeria. The Arabs: A Living History Series. Distributor: Landmark Films. Purchase: $495.**

"The last three films in the Living History Series focus on the processes of post-colonial change in the Arab world. Mahfoud Bennoune analyses the problems faced by Arabs as they constructed their new nations over the past quarter of a century and the solutions open to them. He does so by reference to his own country, Algeria, which achieved its independence in 1962, with appalling loss of life.

"If old ways were obsolete and a new age had to be created in the aftermath of an eight-year war, what industrial and economic options were open to the Algerians?

"Mahfoud Bennoune looks at the process of industrialization and its effect upon a traditional farm and peasant-based economy; its effect upon the quality of day to day life as services and facilities have tried to keep pace with the rush to the cities. Today, housing, education, and transport are all clamouring for attention in a state which has existed, on its own terms, for a mere twenty years. Nevertheless, Algeria has created a path and has followed it, striving to remove the shackles of economic and cultural dependency as once it struggled to remove the colonizers." DIST

The City Victorious? **Written by Galal Amin. Directed by Geoff Dunlop. 1986. 50 minutes. Color film and videocassette. With study guide. Major locations: Cairo, the Nile Delta. The Arabs: A Living History Series. Distributor: Landmark Films. Purchase: $495.**

"This film looks at changing fortunes in the traditional relationship between Arab city and countryside. We focus on one small corner of Cairo and one small village in the Nile Delta, sixty miles to the north. In the village we meet a young peasant, Mitwali Balah, and come to understand his arduous life which he wishes to exchange for the seemingly magical prospects of life in Cairo. The film follows the young man to Cairo where he seeks the advice and company of other migrant workers from his home village. Disillusion sets in and he returns to the Delta.

"The lives of these young peasants are looked at not only in the context of the overburdened, overpopulated Cairo of today, but in the context of a nineteenth century dream, of creating a city to rival Paris. Ever-present are the great monuments of medieval Cairo—a potent reminder of the power that flowed from her when she was the greatest of all Arab cities. In observing the struggles and hopes of the migrant workers, economist Galal Amin shows how the once-dominant Arab city has become simply another metropolis, dependent for its survival on manipulation from afar and social forces which are now universal."DIST

Family Ties. **Written by Nadia Hijab. Directed by Colin Luke. 1986. 50 minutes. Color film and videocassette. With study guide. Major locations: Jordan, Tunisia, Egypt. The Arabs: A Living History Series. Distributor: Landmark Films. Purchase: $495.**

"Most Arab women's lives still center on the family, their traditional responsibilities to their own children and the power of parents and relatives to dictate their role in life.

"Writer and journalist Nadia Hijab weaves this film around a large extended family of Jordanians living in Amman. The mother, Umm Ghassem, is clearly the powerful heart of this family—strong and humorous and frank in her description of her life.

"In spite of its traditional restraints, the extended Arab family is seen to work—as secure and loving and caring as it has always been. But we also meet other girls and women who feel that the traditional role of wife and mother is insufficient—the Tunisian girl who longs to leave home and find her own flat, the modern Jordanian woman who flies a Tri-Star and plays squash to keep fit.

"As she talks to these Arab women and their families and to women active in medicine, politics, literature and the law, Nadia Hijab asks 'How can we Arabs preserve the strengths of our family life and still give women a chance to lead their own lives?' " DIST

From the West Bank to Armageddon: The Direction of U.S. Policy in the Middle East. **Produced by Sara Freedman and Ted German. 1984. Color slideshow with cassette tape. 3 parts. With discussion guide. Distributor: Mobilization for Survival. Rental: $45/week. Also from American Friends Service Committee (Cambridge and San Francisco) and ADC Organizing Dept.**

"Presents a critical, comprehensive overview of U.S. policy in the Middle East, examining in particular the effects of this policy on the Israeli-Palestinian conflict. The slideshow is divided into three sections, each of which can be used independently of the others: (1) 'The Role of

the United States in the Middle East'; (2) 'A Historical Overview of the Palestinian-Israeli Conflict'; and 'The Occupation of the West Bank.'"
DIST

Gaza Ghetto: A Portrait of a Palestinian Refugee Family 1948-84. **Produced by Peä Holmquist, Joan Mandell, and Pierre Björklund. 1984. 82 minutes. Color film and videocassette. Distributor: New Time Films. Rental: $135 (film only). Purchase: $1,500 (film), $750 (video). Also from Icarus Films.**

"In 1948, twenty-year-old Palestinian Abu-el Adel fled with his family as Israeli troops advanced on the village of Dimra. Their flight led them to the Jabalia Refugee Camp in Gaza. Since 1967 Gaza has been occupied by Israeli forces.

"Today, Abu-el Adel passes the ruins of Dimra every morning on his way to Tel Aviv's illegal labor market where Israeli companies hire Palestinian day-laborers. And on the lands of what was once Abu-el Adel's neighboring village, Israeli Minister of Trade and Industry, General Ariel Sharon, is the owner of a flourishing farm. In *Gaza Ghetto,* Gen. Sharon explains why he blew up large sections of the Jabalia Camp in the early 1970's.

"For Abu-el Adel, his daughter Itadhal, her husband Mustapha, and their seven children, life in the Jabalia Camp is characterized by total insecurity — the destruction of houses, curfews, and killings at demonstrations. The film follows them in both joy, the birth of Mukhless, and sorrow, grandmother's funeral." DIST

The Hundred Years War: Personal Notes. **Produced by Ilan Ziv. 1983. Videocassette. Two parts (60 min. each). Distributor: Icarus Films. Rental: $100 each. Purchase: $450 each. Ten percent discount when ordering both.**

"Made over a four year period, *The Hundred Years War* is a sweeping picture of history, changing lives, a war in Lebanon, land occupations and displacements on the West Bank, and of division within the Israeli Jewish community and the rise of Gush Emunim.

"Part 1 begins in Lebanon, but then turns its focus to the West Bank. There it documents the course of Israeli land and labor policies, and the ongoing displacement of Palestinians.

"Part 2 analyzes the impact of Israel's West Bank policies on the political and social development of Israeli society. This part looks closely at Gush Emunim and the rise of the annexationist forces." DIST

In the Footsteps of Abraham. **1985. 27 minutes. Color film and videocassette. 13 programs. Distributor: Landmark Films. Purchase: $475 (film), $375 (video). 13 videos for $4,375.**

"This series of thirteen programs follows the journey that Abraham, the first of the prophets, made some four thousand years ago from Ur to Jerusalem and as far as to Mecca.

"To make this journey again today means discovering all the vitality of Abraham's posterity and the incredible flourishing of spiritual movements affected by thousands of years of religious quarrels, torn apart by internal differences, decimated by persecutions but preserved by geographic accident, movements which all stem from the same common origin." DIST

Iran: A Revolution Betrayed. **Produced by BBC. 1984. 60 minutes. Videocassette. Distributor: Films Incorporated. Rental: $90. Purchase: $298 (¾ inch), $198 (½ inch).**

"This is a diary of events leading up to the Iranian revolution and of the aftermath which turned the country into a seething cauldron of political and religious unrest. It includes Ahsan Adib's clandestinely shot film of dramatic events which shook the streets of Tehran in 1978 and 1979. Adib risked his life to record this film which was smuggled out of Iran." DIST

Iran: A Righteous Republic. **Produced by Tim Hodlin. 1986. 48 minutes. Color film and videocassette. Distributor: Landmark Films. Purchase: $450.**

"Revolutionary Iran has suffered thousands of casualties in the Gulf War, and in internal strife, but for millions of Muslims all over the world it is a model for the future—the only true Islamic Republic and a viable alternative to domination by either West or East.

"Tim Hodlin, an experienced observer of Iran, visited the country and its unique schools for religious and revolutionary training. He has shown the way of life now in Iran, how even with all the casualties there are more and more volunteers to go to the front in the war with Iraq. He also describes the effect that this country with its Quoranic way of life has had on the population of the other Arab countries." DIST

Islam: An Introduction. **22 minutes. Color slideshow with cassette tape. 124 slides with study guide. Distributor: Islamic Affairs Programs of the Middle East Institute. Purchase: $75. Also available in filmstrip, film, and videotape formats. Inquire for rental and purchase fees.**

"A widely distributed multi-media kit designed as a basic introduction to Islam. It includes a twenty-two minute audio-visual presentation and one copy of the printed packet 'Islam: An Introduction.'" DIST

Israeli Settlements: Time Is Running Out. **1983. 20 minutes. Color slideshow with cassette tape. Distributor: American Friends Service Committee (Cambridge). Rental: $15. Also from Mennonite Central Committee (Akron and Alberta offices only).**

"Examines Israeli settlement policy in the West Bank and Gaza Strip. Gives good historical background to the expropriation of Palestinian lands. Focus on U.S. subsidization of the Israeli settlements. Examines Palestinian resistance to Israel's continued expropriation of their land. Looks at Israeli peace movement's opposition to the settlements. Offers ideas for peace terms between Israel and the Palestinians. Lots of useful details." DIST

Jerusalem of Heaven and Earth. **1984. 25 minutes each. Color film and videocassette. 8 programs. Distributor: Landmark Films. Purchase: $450 (film), $99 (video). Entire series: $3,250 (8 films), $750 (8 videos).**

"Jerusalem the Golden, the Holy City, has long inspired painters and poets. Today, it is the bustling and rapidly expanding Capital of the State of Israel, but it has lost none of the fascination or contention that has for so long held the interest of the world. This ambitious eight-part series has covered the full spectrum of this complex city. From the markets of the Old City to the brand new apartment buildings of the rising suburbs; from the Golden Dome of the Rock to the thriving academies of the Orthodox Jews. By meeting and talking to the inheritors of the Jerusalem saga, the people who live and work there, the series looks at what the city has been, what it is now, and what it may become." DIST

Jordan's Stormy Banks: Toward Understanding the Middle East. **Produced by Presbyterian Church (U.S.A.). 1985. 20 minutes. Videocassette. Distributor: EcuFilm. Rental: $10.**

"A twenty-minute color and sound filmstrip which explores the social and religious roots of the ongoing crisis in the Middle East. The monotheism shared by Judaism, Christianity, and Islam is described. The complex history of the Middle East in the twentieth century is outlined, and the course of Arab-Palestinian-Jewish relations is summarized. Designed for adults, the filmstrip has been well received by young people. A permanent resource for churches and schools, for there is no denominational reference in the text." DIST

The Making of the Arabs. **Written by Basim Musallam. Directed by Geoff Dunlop. 1986. 50 minutes. Color film and videocassette. With study guide. Major locations: Lebanon, Egypt, Kuwait, Morocco. The Arabs: A Living History Series. Distributor: Landmark Films. Purchase: $495.**

"This first film in the series 'The Arabs: A Living History' introduces the viewer to the rich variety of life, opinion, and history that exists in the region we call the Arab world—the lands which stretch from the mountains of Morocco to the deserts of the Arabian Peninsula, from the valley of the Nile to the eastern shores of the Mediterranean Sea.

"Why do the 180 million people who inhabit these lands call themselves Arabs? As he journeys through this crucial region Basim Musallam talks to men and women from the four corners of the Arab world and searches for the source of the Arab identity which he and they share. The film starts in his troubled home-city of Beirut; moves to Cairo; to the bustle of Kuwait; to the ancient and beautiful land of Morocco.

"With a rich mixture of historical and living imagery and through the encounters with his own generation of articulate, questioning Arabs, Basim Musallam shows how modern Arab political identity crystallized early in the twentieth century, and how the Arabs drew, as they still draw, on the historical and cultural achievements of their medieval forebears." DIST

Native Sons: Palestinians in Exile. **Produced by Tom Hayes. 1985. Color film. Distributor: Foglight Films. Also from ADC Organizing Department.**

"Three Palestinian families in Badawi and Rashadiya camps in southern Lebanon describe their lives as refugees living a few miles from their homeland." DIST

Nazareth in August. Produced by Norman Cowie, Ahmed Damian, and Dan Walworth. 1986. 58 minutes. Color videocassette. Distributor: Third World Newsreel. Purchase: $300. Rental: $75.

"*Nazareth in August* is a documentary on the Palestinian Arabs within the state of Israel and their efforts, as Israeli citizens, to gain equal rights. This, and other aspects of the Palestinian question, are analyzed in the words of officials, activists, and workers, both Arab and Jewish.

"Nazareth, the largest Arab city in the state, is presented as a metaphor for the remaining Arab towns and villages in Israel and the occupied territories. Surrounded by settlements and the ever-encroaching Jewish city of Nazareth Elite, the continued existence of the fifty-five thousand Arabs of Nazareth remains a struggle.

"Every August since 1976, a voluntary work camp brings together thousands of Nazareth's supporters to help repair and rebuild a city that is systematically underfunded by the state.

"The video weaves its narrative through the streets of Nazareth, Beirut, and New York City. It provides a clear picture of the contradictions at work in Israel and the Middle East today." DIST

New Knowledge for Old. Written by Abdulhamid Sabra. Directed by Geoff Dunlop. 1986. 50 minutes. Color film and videocassette. With study guide. Major locations: Kuwait, Cairo, United States. The Arabs: A Living History Series. Distributor: Landmark Films. Purchase: $495.

"Nine hundred years ago Arab Muslims were the world's greatest seekers after knowledge and wisdom, and the custodians of the scientific wisdom of the Greeks. Today that Arab scholarship is a natural part of the inheritance of all scientists and thinkers—not least of the modern generation of Arab research-workers, many of whom work in the new institutes in the Gulf States which we visit in the course of this film. Abdulhamid Sabra, himself an historian of science, stresses the need for all modern societies to recognize and embrace their own scientific and cultural heritage.

"Only forty years ago Kuwait was predominantly a small community of traders, fishermen, and pearl divers on the Eastern fringe of the Arab world. But there was already the promise of oil. The oil-generated wealth of the past twenty years has transformed Kuwait into a thriving, modern city state with the highest per capita income in the world. It is a place to which scholars and scientists now come to share in the new technological opportunities, and where modern education and research are pursued with vigor." DIST

Nothing Quiet on the Southern Front. 1985. 30 minutes. Color slideshow with cassette tape. Distributor: American Friends Service Committee (Cambridge). Rental: $15.

"Describes the conflicts on NATO's Southern Front—in the Middle East and North Africa. Portrays U.S. and Soviet intervention in the region and the possible nuclear war consequences of that intervention. Produced by European peace activists from a European frame of reference on the crisis in the area." DIST

On Our Land: Palestinians under Israeli Rule. **Produced by Antonia Caccia. 1981. Color film and videocassette. Distributor: Icarus Films. Rental: $100 (film only). Purchase: $865 (film), $550 (video). Also from IDERA Films.**

"One out of every six Israeli citizens is a Palestinian Arab. Originally a peasant farming community, they have lost most of their land to Israeli kibbutz and moshav settlements, and have been turned into wage laborers commuting to Israel's cities or working on Israel's farms. Compared to other Israeli citizens they have been discriminated against in housing, employment, and education.

"This films centers on Umm el-Fahm, the largest Arab village inside Israel. Through portrayal of daily life in the village, and contrasting conditions there with those in settlements built on land that used to belong to Umm el-Fahm, *On Our Land* tells the story of this forgotten section of the Palestinian population." DIST

The Power of the Word. **Written by Khalida Said. Directed by Colin Luke. 1986. 50 minutes. Color film and videocassette. With study guide. Major locations: South Yemen, North Yemen, Syria, Lebanon. The Arabs: A Living History Series. Distributor: Landmark Films. Purchase: $495.**

"The ancient Arabic language, transplanted, with the spread of Islam, from the Arabian Peninsula to Europe and the borders of China, remains the pivot of Arab culture today.

"Arabic, the language of the Quran, is the sacred language for all Muslims and has played a major role in shaping and maintaining Arab society. Poetry remains the forum for political debate, and major poets attract thousands to hear them recite their latest works.

"In the words of writer Khalida Said: 'Poetry is the best witness to our crisis — it's our creative response to these bad times.' Paradoxically, war-torn Lebanon is a meeting place of contemporary intellectual thought in the Arab world; still the publishing center, still a refuge for poets, painters, and novelists from troubled Arab lands: 'the capital of the Arabs' deepest wounds.'

"We discover poets and the origins of poetry, actors and the origins of Arab theatre; but above all this is a film about how Arab writers respond to the challenges of the modern world." DIST

The Price of Change. **Produced by Elizabeth Fernea and Marilyn Gaunt. 1982. 26 minutes. Color film and videocassette. A study guide by Elizabeth Fernea accompanies the film. $55 (film only). Distributor: Icarus Films. Rental: $470 (film), $260 (video). Also from IDERA Films.**

"For sixty years Egyptian women have been gradually entering all sectors of the public workforce. Work outside the home, once considered shameful, has become a necessity. Today, nearly forty percent of Egyptian women contribute in some way to providing the family income.

"*The Price of Change* examines the consequences of work for five women — a factory worker, a village leader involved with family planning, a doctor, a social worker, and a member of Parliament.

"The film presents a picture of changing attitudes towards work, the family, sex, and women's place in Egyptian society." DIST

The Shadow of the West. **Written by Edward Said. Directed by Geoff Dunlop. 1986. 50 minutes. Color film and videocassette. With study guide. Major locations: Lebanon, Israel, United States. The Arabs: A Living History Series. Distributor: Landmark Films. Purchase: $495.**

"This film assesses the changes which came about as the Arab countries were drawn into the new political and economic order of modern times. Those changes not only affected the Arab countries, but also the way in which they came to be viewed by people in Europe and America.

"Its main focus is on the plight of the Palestinians, which can be seen as the most enduring residue of the modern encounter between the Arabs and the West.

"Edward Said is a Palestinian living and working in New York. He is outspokenly and actively critical of the treatment of his fellow-Palestinians and is no longer welcome in the city of his birth, Jerusalem. In this film Said develops the themes contained in his trilogy of books: *Orientalism, The Question of Palestine,* and *Covering Islam.* He traces the course of European involvement with the Near East from a vision of the Holy Land, via the Crusades, to Napoleon's campaign in Egypt in 1799 and the French and British entrepreneurs, adventurers, and empire-builders who came in his wake." DIST

Shots of Conflict: Report from South Lebanon. **Produced by AFSC and the National Council of Churches (USA). 1985. Color slideshow with cassette tape. Distributor: American Friends Service Committee (Cambridge). Rental: $15.**

"Provides an overview of the general situation in southern Lebanon from the 1982 Israeli invasion up through 1984. Powerful, provocative, and fair." DIST

Shrine under Siege. **Produced by Ilan Ziv. 1985. 42 minutes. Videocassette. Distributor: Icarus Films. Rental: $60. Purchase: $350.**

"*Shrine under Siege* explores the connection between Fundamentalist Christians in the United States and militant Jews in Israel to destroy Islam's third holiest shrine, the Haram Ash-Sharif (the Dome of the Rock), and build in its place the Third Jewish Temple.

"The documentary explores the theological background for this unusual coalition, and places it within the political context—the increased political power of fundamentalism in the United States, and the rise of extremist religious parties in Israel symbolized by the election to Parliament of Rabbi Meir Kahane.

"*Shrine under Siege* shows that what might seem to some an esoteric religious fantasy is in fact a dangerous new element of the Middle East conflict." DIST

The Society of the Just. **Produced by Francois Bardet and George Marty. 1986. 56 minutes. Videocassette. Distributor: Landmark Films. Purchase: $450. Rental: $45.**

"Forty million inhabitants, one million square miles, major oil producer, strategic location—Iran, today's international villain.

"Producer George Marty lived in Tehran for many years and witnessed the events of the past two decades firsthand. One of the most informed Iran-specialists today, he gives us a subtle analysis of the political, historical, social, and economic situation in the Islamic Republic, a rare look behind the well-known facade of violence and fanaticism. Marty's talks with Dr. Shams Ardekani, a close advisor to Khomeini, with Ayatollah Nouri, one of the leading ideologists for the regime, with Dr. Behrouzi, a woman deputy to the Parliament, with Mr. Rafighdoust, the minister of the Revolutionary Guards, and with others, reveal a national sense of identity which often disappears behind the image of fist-shaking crowds." DIST

Terrorism and the Gospel. **Produced by Presbyterian Peacemaking Program. 1986. 90 minutes. Videocassette. 6-session program, with leader's guide. Distributor: Kerr Associates. Purchase: $49.95. Extra copies of student book are available for $1.95 each.**

"*Terrorism and the Gospel* is a 90-minute, six-session video-based 'happening' in which the experiences, reflections, and courageous faith of Ben and Carol Weir are the basis for creative classroom interaction.

"The Rev. Benjamin Weir, currently Moderator of the Presbyterian Church (U.S.A.), was taken hostage and chained almost constantly to a radiator in the small room in Lebanon where he was held captive for eighteen months. He used his imprisonment as a time of deep spiritual reflection and, in the *Terrorism and the Gospel* video tape, he shares these reflections in a way which helps participants deal with the prisons in their own lives.

"Carol Weir witnessed the kidnapping of her husband and feared for his safety. As she dealt emotionally and spiritually with what had happened, she felt the strong support of Lebanese friends and neighbors as a caring community developed around her. Her powerful story on the *Terrorism and the Gospel* video tape is a witness to the kind of strength which comes from Christian faith and human interaction.

"The events of the hostage months are gradually revealed as the Weirs reflect on the meaning of the Garden of Gethsemane narrative. . . . The video tape and student book lead participants through the specific situations of Ben and Carol Weir to a broader understanding of the crises in the Middle East, to an awareness that all of the participants in the Middle East struggle are children of God, and to a bold commitment to peacemaking through the extension of God's love to all persons." DIST

Time Is Running Out for an Israeli-Palestinian Peace. **Produced by AFSC International Division. 1983. 35 minutes. Color slideshow with cassette tape. Distributor: American Friends Service Committee (San Francisco). Rental: $20.**

"The increasing number of Israeli settlements in the occupied territories of the West Bank and Gaza have led to divisions between Israelis and Palestinians as well as among Israelis themselves. This show looks at the increasing tensions associated with that process and examines what can be done to reverse it." DIST

Under a Crescent Moon. **Produced by Seventh Art Productions. 1987. 52 minutes. Videocassette. Distributor: Landmark Films. Purchase: $295.**

"This vivid documentary film captures the visual splendor of Islamic Africa. Set in the ancient city of Kano on the southern edge of the Sahara, the film portrays a historic and fascinating society revealed through the Sallah Festival marking the end of the Ramadan fast.

"Kano was visited over a thousand years ago by Berber merchants in search of gold and precious commodities from the African interior. The Berbers brought with them the teachings of Mohamad which became the basis of a culture and way of life which prevail to this day.

"*Under a Crescent Moon* pays particular attention to Kano's Islamic ruler — the emir — throughout the festival. We take a privileged look behind the fifteenth-century baked-earth walls of his elaborate palace encountering court musicians and entering normally forbidden women's quarters. From the palace we move to the prayer ground where the emir joins hundreds of thousands of his subjects in prostrate praise to Allah. The festival ends dramatically. Fiercely adorned warrior horsemen brandishing their weapons make a series of charges. Within inches of the monarch the horses are dragged back on their haunches as a final show of deference.

"*Under a Crescent Moon* is a visually and musically captivating film revealing Islam as a live force in Africa."

Under Siege: Palestinians in the U.S. Media. **Videocassette. Distributor: Paper Tiger TV. Rental: $50. Purchase: $100. Program no. 108.**

"Rashid Khalidi looks at terrorism, the media and the history of Palestine. Rashid Khalidi teaches Middle Eastern history at Columbia University." DIST

A Veiled Revolution. **Produced by Elizabeth Fernea and Marilyn Gaunt. 1982. 26 minutes. Color film and videocassette. With study guide by Elizabeth Fernea. Distributor: Icarus Films. Rental: $55 (film only). Purchase: $470 (film), $260 (video). Also from IDERA Films.**

"Egypt was the first Arab country where women marched in political demonstrations (1919); the first where women took off the veil (1923); and the first to offer free public secular education to women (1924). Today the granddaughters of those early Arab feminists are returning to traditional garb, sometimes with full face veil and gloves, which they call Islamic dress.

"What are the reasons for this new movement? Is it an echo of the Iranian revolution? Is it a rejection of Western values? What do women themselves say about it? *A Veiled Revolution* looks at some of this history, and attempts to answer some of these questions." DIST

Ways of Faith. **Written by Ali el Mek. Directed by Geoff Dunlop. 1986. 50 minutes. Color film and videocassette. With study guide. Location: Sudan. The Arabs: A Living History Series. Distributor: Landmark Films. Purchase: $495.**

"Muslim author and poet Ali el Mek looks at the ways and meaning of the Islamic Faith as they affect one particular group of Muslims within his own experience—the people of the village of Umduban in central Sudan. No single community or village can ever adequately represent the entire Islamic Faith, but this encounter with the religious life of Umduban leads to an understanding of that living Islam which informs the very existence of Muslims the world over." DIST

Women under Siege. **1982. Color film and videocassette. Distributor: Icarus Films. Rental: $50 (film only). Purchase: $425 (film), $260 (video). Also from IDERA Films.**

"Rashadiyah is a town six miles north of the Israeli border, in Southern Lebanon. Once a peaceful agricultural village, in 1964 it became the setting for a camp housing 14,000 Palestinian refugees. For years they lived under constant harassment and threat of Israeli attack.

"Women play a crucial role in the Palestinian community, as mothers, teachers, political organizers, farm laborers, and fighters. Through actual footage and interviews with the women of Rashadiyah, this film explores the lives of six representative Palestinian women.

"In June 1982, Rashadiyah was bombed and attacked by Israeli forces. The camp was reduced to ruins, many of the residents were forced to flee again." DIST

SUPPLEMENTARY LIST OF VISUAL RESOURCES

MIDDLE EAST GENERAL

American Foreign Policy. Produced by Creative Communications/Encyclopaedia Britannica. 1981. 17 minutes. Black and white film. With guide. Distributor: University of Minnesota Audio Visual. Rental: $13. Order no. 4HO971.

Arab Stereotypes in America. Produced by Warren David. 25 minutes. Color slideshow with script. Distributor: Arab-American Media Society. Also from ADC Organizing Department.

The Descent of the Hordes. Produced by David Paradine Films. 1978. 58 minutes. Color film and videocassette. Distributor: Cinema Guild. Rental: $90. Purchase: $795 (film), $495 (video). Crossroads of Civilization Series.

Guardians of the Sacred Flame. Produced by David Paradine Films 1978. 58 minutes. Color film and videocassette. Distributor: Cinema Guild. Rental: $90. Purchase: $795 (film), $495 (video). Crossroads of Civilization Series.

Half the World. Produced by David Paradine Films. 1978. 58 minutes. Color film and videocassette. Distributor: Cinema Guild. Rental: $90. Purchase: $795 (film), $495 (video). Crossroads of Civilization Series.

Heroes or History? Produced by David Paradine Films. 1978. 58 minutes. Color film and videocassette. Distributor: Cinema Guild. Rental: $90. Purchase: $795 (film), $495 (video). Crossroads of Civilization Series.

The Middle East from Mohammed to Sadat. Produced by Educational Audio Visual, Inc. Videocassette. Distributor: Guidance Associates. Purchase: $179. Order no. 05449–860.

Mosaic of Peoples. 1978. 22 minutes. Color film and videocassette. Distributor: Guidance Associates. Rental: $60. Purchase: $515 (film), $280 (video). Order no. 3949.

Noam Chomsky Reads The New York Times: The Middle East. Videocassette. Distributor: Paper Tiger TV. Rental: $50. Purchase: $100. Program no. 88.

Origins and Evidence. Produced by David Paradine Films. 1978. 58 minutes. Color film and videocassette. Distributor: Cinema Guild. Rental: $90. Purchase: $795 (film), $495 (video). Crossroads of Civilization Series.

The Predators. Produced by David Paradine Films. 1978. 58 minutes. Color film and videocassette. Distributor: Cinema Guild. Rental: $90. Purchase: $795 (film), $495 (video). Crossroads of Civilization Series.

The Seventies. Produced by Upitin Documentaries/Journal Films. 1980. 27 minutes. Color film. Distributor: University of Minnesota Audio Visual. Rental: $15.50. Middle East Series. Order no. 7HO977.

Shadow of God on Earth. Produced by David Paradine Films. 1978. 58 minutes. Color film and videocassette. Distributor: Cinema Guild. Rental: $90. Purchase: $795 (film), $495 (video). Crossroads of Civilization Series.

ARABIAN PENINSULA AND GULF

The Petrodollar Coast. Produced by Jo Franklin-Trout. 1983. 52 minutes. Color film. The Oil Kingdoms Series. Distributor: Films Incorporated.

A Sea of Conflict. Produced by Jo Franklin-Trout. 1983. 52 minutes. Color film. The Oil Kingdoms Series. Distributor: Films Incorporated.

FERTILE CRESCENT

The Alien's Place. Produced by Rudolf van den Berg. 1979. 87 minutes. Color film. Distributor: Icarus Films. Rental: $100. Purchase: $1250.

Barricades: Lebanon's Civil War. Produced by Thames Television. 1986. 52 minutes. Color film and videocassette. Distributor: Media Guild. Rental: $65. Purchase: $795 (film), $395 (video).

Between the River and the Sea. 1986. 64 minutes. Color film and videocassette. Distributor: Landmark Films. Purchase: $500.

Building a Dream. 1978. 22 minutes. Color film and videocassette. Distributor: Guidance Associates. Rental: $60. Purchase: $515 (film), $280 (video). Order no. 3950.

Children of Palestine. Produced by Monica Maurer and Samir Nimer

for the Palestine Cinema Institute & Red Crescent. 1979. 35 minutes.
Color film. Distributor: Icarus Films.

Holy Land. Produced by NBC. 1973. 60 minutes. Color film. Distributor: EcuFilm. Rental: $40.

Israel: Crossroads of History. Produced by Pathescope Educational
Media. Color filmstrip with cassette tape. 6 parts, teacher's guide,
library kit. Distributor: Guidance Associates. Purchase: $189. Order
no. 07961–860.

Lebanon: MCC Update. Produced by Mennonite Central Committee.
1985. Color slideshow with script. Distributor: Mennonite Central
Committee. Rental: Free. All offices.

Lebanon Fights for Her Future. Produced by Grassroots International.
1985. 122 minutes. Videocassette. Study guide and resource materials. Distributor: Grassroots International. Also from ADC Organizing Department.

The Massacre and the Masquerade. 58 minutes. Videocassette. Distributor: American-Arab Anti-Discrimination Committee. Rental: $20.

A Morning in Sabra-Shatila Camp. 1982. 20 minutes. Color slideshow
with cassette tape. Distributor: Palestine Human Rights Campaign.

Palestine. Produced by BBC/Thames Television. 1978. Color film and
videocassette. 3 parts. Distributor: Media Guild. Rental: $75. Purchase: $1100 (film), $660 (video).

Palestine Is the Issue. Produced by Allen Carr and Jeanne Carr. 45
minutes. Color filmstrip with cassette tape. Distributor: Association
of Arab-American University Graduates.

Palestine with a Human Face: The Israeli Occupation of the West Bank.
Produced by AAUG and Global Village Associates. 80 minutes. Videocassette. 2 parts. Distributor: Association of Arab-American University Graduates.

The Palestinian People Do Have Rights. Produced by United Nations
Films. 1979. 48 minutes. Color film and videocassette. Distributor:
Icarus Films. Rental: $75. Purchase: $645 (film), $480 (video). Also
from American Friends Service Committee (Cambridge).

Palestinian Refugees in Lebanon. Produced by Roger Pic. 1975. 36
minutes. Color film and videocassette. Distributor: Icarus Films.
Rental: $70 (film only). Purchase: $630 (film), $360 (video).

Paratroopers. Produced by Yehuda Ne'eman. 1976. 95 minutes. Color
film. Distributor: Icarus Films. Rental: $100 (anamorphic lens required). Purchase: $1250.

People Still Live Here. Produced by AFSC and the National Council of
Churches (USA). 14 minutes. Color filmstrip with cassette tape. 80
frames. Distributor: American Friends Service Committee.

To Live in Freedom. Produced by Simon Louvish. 1975. 54 minutes.
Color film. Distributor: Icarus Films. Rental: $100. Purchase: $860.

The Twenty-Third Cease Fire. Produced by Anne Papillaut et al. 1976.
52 minutes. Color film. Distributor: Icarus Films. Rental: $90. Purchase: $830.

The War in Lebanon: An Inside View. Produced by Mya Schone and Ralph Schoenman. Color slideshow with cassette tape. 140 slides. Distributor: Committee for the Defense of the Palestinian and Lebanese People.

What Is MCC West Bank? Produced by Mennonite Central Committee. 1983. 11 minutes. Color slideshow with cassette tape. Distributor: Mennonite Central Committee. Rental: Free. All offices except Great Lakes and Manitoba.

Zahrat El Kindoul: Women from South Lebanon. Produced by Jean Chamoun and Mai Masri. 1986. 71 minutes. Color film and videocassette. Distributor: Palestine Human Rights Campaign. Purchase: $65. Video rental from Arab World Consultants.

NORTH AFRICA

Faces of Egypt. Produced by Phoenix Films. 1981. 26 minutes. Color film. Distributor: Phoenix Films.

Factories for the Third World: Tunisia. Produced by Gordian Troeller and Marie Claude Deffarge. 1979. 43 minutes. Color film and videocassette. Distributor: Icarus Films. Rental: $85. Purchase: $695 (film), $420 (video).

Leadership and Identity. 1978. 22 minutes. Color film and videocassette. Distributor: Guidance Associates. Rental: $60. Purchase: $515 (film), $280 (video). Order no. 3948.

Mudhorse. 1971. 12 minutes. Black and white film. Distributor: Icarus Films. Rental: $25. Purchase: $195.

Sad Song of Touha. 1971. 12 minutes. Black and white film. Distributor: Icarus Films. Rental: $25. Purchase: $195.

Sadat's Eternal Egypt. Produced by CBS/Carousel Films. 1980. 45 minutes. Color film. Distributor: University of Minnesota Audio Visual. Rental: $25. Order no. 1S1893.

Saints and Spirits. Produced by Elizabeth Fernea and Marilyn Davies for Granada Television. 1979. 26 minutes. Color film and videocassette. Distributor: Icarus Films. Rental: $55 (film only). Purchase: $470 (film), $260 (video).

Some Women of Marra Kesh. Produced by Elizabeth Fernea and Marilyn Davies for Granada Television. 1976. 52 minutes. Color film. Distributor: Icarus Films.

The Temptation of Power. Produced by Gordian Troeller and Marie Claude Deffarge. 1977. 43 minutes. Color film and videocassette. Distributor: Icarus Films. Rental: $75 (film only). Purchase: $650 (film), $420 (video).

ISLAM

The Peoples of Islam. Produced by Stuart Day. 1982. 24 minutes. Color film. Distributor: Islamic Affairs Programs of the Middle East Institute.

The Traditional World of Islam. Produced by Exxon Corp. 1976. 156 minutes. Color film. 6 parts (26 min. each). Distributor: ADC Organizing Department. Rental: $50.

The Way of Islam. Produced by Church Missionary Society. 1975. 19 minutes. Color filmstrip with cassette tape. Distributor: Mennonite Central Committee. Rental: Free. Available from Akron and British Columbia offices only.

INFORMATION SOURCES

For information on additional visual resources on the Middle East, see the following directories:

The Middle East and North Africa on Film: An Annotated Filmography. Ed. Marsha Hamilton McClintock. New York: Garland Publishing Co., 1982. 562pp. $50.

This is an exhaustive library reference catalog of more than two thousand films on the Middle East and North Africa. Annotations are brief. Rental sources are given.

A Resource Guide to Materials on the Arab World. Comp. Audrey Shabbas. Belmont, Mass.: Association of Arab-American University Graduates, forthcoming 1987.

This guide is the most comprehensive and up-to-date catalog of audiovisual and curriculum materials on the Middle East. Each entry is annotated, and complete and accurate ordering information is provided.

World of Islam: Images and Echoes. A Critical Guide to Films and Recordings. New York: American Council of Learned Societies, 1980. $9.50.

This guide contains critical evaluations of 237 16MM films for the senior high school and college level. Rental and purchase sources are given. *World of Islam* also includes an annotated catalog of recordings compiled by Lorraine Sakata.

See also the 82-page "Middle East Film Sampler" compiled by Charlotte F. Albright and Ellen-Fairbanks Bodman in *A Resource Guide for Middle Eastern Studies* (see books chapter above).

Two standard library reference guides on audiovisuals are: *Educational Film Locator* from Bowker and Co. (New York) and *The Motion Picture Guide* from CineBooks (Des Moines, Iowa). For an annotated list of films on the Third World (divided into regional chapters), see Helen W. Cyr's *A Filmography of the Third World, 1976-1983* (Metuchen, N.J.: Scarecrow Press, 1985. 275pp. $20. Cloth).

The winter 1986 issue of *Third World Resources* contained a four-page, fully annotated information guide to sources of information on

Third World audiovisuals (50 cents, from Third World Resources, 464 19 St., Oakland, CA 94612). See the other publications from **Third World Resources,** described in the preface to this resource directory.

AUDIO RESOURCES

Information in the **annotated entries** is given in the following order: title; artist(s) or producer(s); date; length; format (record or tape); distributor; ordering number; price; and descripton of content.

As with the visual resources, the DIST code at the end of the annotation indicates that the description of the record or tape is the distributor's. Annotations that are not within quotation marks are our own.

Audio resources in the **supplementary list** (pp. 120–121) are grouped under these headings: Middle East general; Fertile Crescent; North Africa; Islam; Iran; and Turkey.

The **information sources** section (p. 121) provides information on catalogs that contain the names of other audio resources related to the Middle East.

ANNOTATED ENTRIES

Andah Aleik. **Wardah. Long-playing record or cassette tape. Distributor: Ladyslipper. Order no.: Soutelphan 150 (record), C-150 (tape). $9.95.**

"A live recording by a vocalist who, originally from Algeria and now residing in Cairo, is well-loved in the Arab world and has around fifty recordings to her credit." DIST

The Arab-Israeli Conflict. **James Fine. 1981. 30 minutes. Cassette tape. Distributor: Great Atlantic Radio Conspiracy. Order no.: 24–381–318. $5 (individuals), $8.50 (institutions).**

"Throughout the twentieth century a bitter struggle has pervaded the Middle East. The Jewish and Zionist communities on the one side and the Palestinian Arabs on the other have been fighting to establish their national identity in the same territory. American Friends Service Committee Middle East field director James Fine talks about the conflict." DIST

Conversations from the Middle East. Produced by Sarah Jacobus. 1984. 90 minutes. Cassette tape. Distributor: Pacifica Radio Archive. Order no.: SZ0259.01, 02, and 03. $11 each.

"Three candid and personal interviews with women of different cultures in the Middle East, recorded on location in Israel and the Golan Heights. These programs weave the women's stories with music and ambient sound." DIST

The Days of Fakhr Eddeen. Fairuz. Long-playing record. Distributor: Monitor Recordings. Order no.: 707. $8.98.

"The top performer of Lebanon sings highlights from a musical play concerning the fate of Lebanese patriots in the seventeenth century, at a time when they were in constant risk of domination by foreign powers." DIST

Dov Yirmiya. Produced by David Barsamian. 1985. 30 minutes. Cassette tape. Distributor: Pacifica Radio Archive. Order no.: SZ0285. $11.

"Dov Yirmiya is an Israeli war hero and author of *My War Diary*, an account of his experiences during the Israeli invasion of Lebanon. Because of his public criticism of the invasion, he was forced to resign from the army. Yirmiya, who was born in Palestine, gives an historical perspective of Israel from the early Zionists to the present. He talks about the possibility of reconciliation and peace between Israelis and Palestinians." DIST

The Economics of Occupation: Agriculture on the West Bank. Produced by Nadia Yaqub. 1984. 29 minutes. Cassette tape. Distributor: Pacifica Radio Archive. Order no.: AZ0774. $11.

"With 80 percent of Palestinians on the West Bank living in rural areas, agriculture is the mainstay of the West Bank economy. Israeli restrictions on Palestinian agriculture have a profound effect on the economy. This documentary is taken from interviews with Palestinians and Israelis in the occupied territories. Examined are the conditions of West Bank agriculture, the effect of Israeli restrictions, and the implications of a stunted Palestinian economy for a future independent state." DIST

Edward Said: The Idea of Palestine. 1982. 32 minutes. Cassette tape. Distributor: Pacifica Radio Archive. Order no.: KZ1147.08. $13.

"Edward Said, professor from Columbia University and author of *The Question of Palestine*, claims that it is the idea of Palestine which the Israelis are fighting. He also describes the resistance of the Palestinians, how it is the focus for all Arabs, and the realities of present Israeli policies." DIST

Elon Halavi. 1984. 28 minutes. Cassette tape. Distributor: Pacifica Radio Archive. Order no.: AZ0881. $11.

KPFA's lawyer Maldari "interviews Elon Halavi, the Palestinian Liberation Organization's delegate to the 1984 Socialist International. Halavi, a Sephardic Jew, worked for many years as a peace activist inside Israel. He holds dual French and Israeli citizenship and now represents the PLO. In this interview he describes the evolution of his personal and political beliefs as well as giving a succinct analysis of Zionism, anti-semitism, and racism in the Middle East." DIST

Eyes on the Horizon: The Quest for Peace in the Middle East. **Produced by Helene Rosenbluth and Sarah Jacobus. 1983. 29 minutes. Cassette tape. Distributor: Pacifica Radio Archive. Order no.: KZ1334. $11.**

"Profiles the people working on a grassroots level for a peaceful resolution of the complex Middle East conflict. Interviews with members of Israel's diverse peace groups and Palestinian activists on the West Bank are interwoven with the sounds and music of Israel and the West Bank." DIST

Felicia Langer. **1984. 29 minutes. Cassette tape. Distributor: Pacifica Radio Archive. Order no.: AZ0770. $11.**

An interview with "Felicia Langer, prominent Israeli lawyer who is Vice President of the Israeli League for Civil and Human Rights. Ms. Langer discusses violations of civil and human rights on the Israeli occupied West Bank. She was the first Israeli attorney to charge government police with the violation of Palestinian prisoners' human rights. She also discusses the defense of Palestinians, Israeli public opinion regarding human and civil rights, the incidence of torture, and the role of U.S. peace activists." DIST

Iran. **Gary G. Sick. Produced by the Johnson Foundation. 1986. 30 minutes. Cassette tape. Conversations from Wingspread Series. Distributor: the Johnson Foundation. Order no.: R-1265. $4.**

"Former Carter White House aide, a participant in a Wingspread conference on educating Americans about international affairs, sponsored by the Council on Foundations and the Johnson Foundation, who authored *All Fall Down*, a major book about the Iranian Revolution and hostage crisis, discusses Iran as a friend and ally of the U.S. under the Shah, and examines the chain of events that led to the revolution and take-over by the Ayatollah Khomeini, the hostage crisis, and the trade, terrorist, and diplomatic events of recent times. The possible future events and future leadership of Iran which may come about are explored. Iran under a theocratic system and the strengths and weaknesses of that kind of system are discussed. Iran as a supporter of terrorism as well as a target of terrorism is described. Possible lessons and changes in U.S. foreign policy toward Iran are considered." DIST

Letters from Beirut. **1985. 30 minutes. Cassette tape. Distributor: Pacifica Radio Archive. Order no.: AZ0791. $11.**

"Through interviews with residents of Lebanon and letters from inhabitants of Beirut who lived through the 1982 invasion of Lebanon, Nadia Yaqub takes a personal look at the siege and the U.S. role in the war." DIST

Nairobi Women's Conference: A Palestinian Perspective. **Camelia Odeh. Produced by Still Mad Collective. 1985. 33 minutes. Cassette tape. Distributor: Pacifica Radio Archive. Order no.: AZ0831. $13.**

"Camelia Odeh describes her experience as one of the Palestinian

AUDIOVISUALS

delegates to the 1985 United Nations Women's Conference. She talks about conference presentations on the conditions of Palestinian women's lives in Israel, and the unity being developed between Palestinians and progressive Israeli Jews. She describes people working together for peace in South Africa, Central America, and the Middle East." DIST

Noam Chomsky: U.S. Intervention in Latin America and the Middle East. **Produced by David Barsamian. 1984. 76 minutes. Cassette tape. Distributor: Pacifica Radio Archive. Order no.: SZ0223. $15.**

"Controversial political activist and professor of linguistics at MIT, Noam Chomsky describes the historical context and ideology that underlies U.S. intervention around the world. Particular emphasis is placed on Latin America and the Middle East. Using existing U.S. Government planning documents, he offers explanations for the correlations between human rights violations and the investment climate for American business." DIST

Palestine Lives. **Long-playing record. Distributor: Paredon Records. Order no.: P-1022. $8.**

"Songs of national liberation from the struggle of the people of Palestine sung by guerrilla fighters accompanied by traditional instruments. Recorded by Al Fatah." DIST

A Palestinian-Israeli Dialogue. **Mary Khass and Lisa Blume. Produced by Helene Rosenbluth. 1985. 60 minutes. Cassette tape. Distributor: Pacifica Radio Archive. Order no.: KZ1401. $13.**

"The 1985 U.N. International Women's Conference in Nairobi was heated and explosive. This Forum '85 session brought together Israelis, Palestinians, Jews, and Arabs from all over the world in continued dialogue to achieve better understanding. Mary Khass, a Palestinian activist from Golan, and Lisa Blume, a vocal member of the Israeli Peace Now Movement, engage in a moving process of sharing commonalities, airing differences and working toward peace in their homeland. Historic." DIST

Promises of the Storm. **Marcel Khalifé. 1985. Long-playing record. Distributor: Paredon Records. $8, plus $1.50 postage.**

"Combining the widely acclaimed artistry of Marcel Khalifé with the poetry of Mahmoud Darwish and Izzidine Al Munassrah, this record embodies the cultural ferment of the Arab world today. These artists explore their people's roots and traditions while critically examining and confronting the immensity of the struggles before them—an accomplishment representing a reality Israeli tanks have not been able to crush.

"Deeply influenced by traditional Arabic music, Khalifé has greatly modernized and expanded the use of the *oud,* a distant cousin of the lute and a cornerstone of Arabic music. He brings poetry to life, much the way Arab troubadours of old enhanced and enlivened their own legends.

"The work of these artists woven together embodies the strength of two peoples—Lebanese and Palestinian—who have the resolve to control their own destinies. As one example of the rich culture produced by this powerful, passionate, and moving goal, *Promises of the Storm* is offered as a tribute to two peoples who sing songs of hope and resistance amidst the ashes of Beirut." DIST

Terrorism: The Sacred Rage. **Robin Wright. Produced by the Johnson Foundation. 1986. 30 minutes. Cassette tape. Conversations from Wingspread Series. Distributor: the Johnson Foundation. Order no.: R-1219. $4.**

"A briefing convened by the Johnson Foundation. This program deals with the roots of terrorism in an interview with Robin Wright, author of *Sacred Rage: The Wrath of Militant Islam.* Areas covered include a description of Islam as a religion in which politics and religion are inseparable, Islam as religion which does not promote or condone terrorism and violence, the exception of the Shiites, the deteriorating relationship between Islam and the West, U.S. actions which have provoked the Muslim world, the role of oil and U.S. interest in the Middle East, the negative response of Muslims to westernization, religion as increasing world force, emergence of moderates in Iran, need for U.S. to evaluate history and apply to the future, the U.S. and *scapegoat* mentality in these matters, impact of U.S. air strike on Libya, as turning point in our relationship with Arab and Muslim world, problems with defining terrorism, need to learn how to deal with root causes of terrorism, the two causes for Middle East violence as residing in the Palestinian dispute and the collision of the West with militant Islam, importance for U.S. to move toward diffusing of tension with Iran, and need for thoughtful rather than passionate U.S. policy." DIST

The United States and Israel: A Master-Client Relationship. **1985. 90 minutes. Cassette tape. Distributor: Pacifica Radio Archive. Order no.: SZ0277. $15.**

"Noam Chomsky, professor of linguistics at MIT, talks about the material, diplomatic, and ideological underpinnings of U.S.-Israel relations. He sees Washington as police headquarters and Israel as the cop on the beat enforcing U.S. interests. Chomsky believes that if the U.S. continues its current relationship with Israel, and if Israel should decide not to agree to support U.S. interests, then Israel will be left in a perilously vulnerable position." DIST

Women of the Arab World: Nawal Al-Saadawi. **Produced by Nancy Delaney. 1984. 59 minutes. Cassette tape. Distributor: Pacifica Radio Archive. Order no.: AZ0839.**

"Saadawi, an Egyptian psychiatrist, talks about the impact of religion, economics and cultural value-conflicts on the Arab woman's efforts to develop her own life from ancient Egypt to the present. She assaults the stereotypes of Arab women and the emphasis on religion as a person's primary identification. She also looks at the process of westernization many say is happening among Arab women." DIST

SUPPLEMENTARY LIST OF AUDIO RESOURCES

MIDDLE EAST GENERAL

Arabic and Druse Music. Long-playing record. Ethnic Series. Distributor: Folkways. Order no.: 4480. $10.98.
Arabic Songs of Lebanon and Egypt. Long-playing record. International Series. Distributor: Folkways. Order no.: 6925. $9.98.

FERTILE CRESCENT

Afif Bulus Sings Songs of Lebanon, Syria, and Jordan. Long-playing record. International Series. Distributor: Folkways. Order no.: 8816. $9.98.
Bedouin Music of South Sinai. Long-playing record. Ethnic Series. Distributor: Folkways. Order no.: 4204. $10.98.
Folk Music of Palestine. Long-playing record. Ethnic Series. Distributor: Folkways. Order no.: 4408. $10.98.
Hebrew Folk Songs. Mark Olf. Long-playing record. International Series. Distributor: Folkways. Order no.: 6928. $9.98.
The Shiites of Lebanon. Abbas H. Hamdani. Produced by the Johnson Foundation. 1985. 30 minutes. Cassette tape. Conversations from Wingspread Series. Distributor: the Johnson Foundation. Order no.: R-1153. $4.
Songs of Israel. Hillel and Aviva. Long-playing record. International Series. Distributor: Folkways. Order no.: 6847. $9.98.
Songs of Jerusalem. Long-playing record. International Series. Distributor: Folkways. Order no.: 8552. $9.98.
The Very Best of Fairuz. Long-playing record or cassette tape. Distributor: Ladyslipper. Order no.: Voix de l'Orient 241 (record), C-241 (tape). $9.95.
Yemenite and Other Israeli Folk Songs. Geula Gill. Dov Seltzer Group. Long-playing record. International Series. Distributor: Folkways. Order no.: 8735. $9.98.

NORTH AFRICA

Islam. Yvonne Yazbeck Haddad. Produced by the Johnson Foundation. 1984. 30 minutes. Cassette tape. Conversations from Wingspread Series. Distributor: the Johnson Foundation. Order no.: R-1030. $4.
Music of Algeria. Long-playing record. Ethnic Series. Distributor: Folkways. Order no.: 4341. $10.98.
Music of Morocco. Long-playing record. Ethnic Series. Distributor: Folkways. Order no.: 4339. $10.98.

Tunisia. Long-playing record. 3 vols. International Series. Distributor: Folkways. Order no.: 8861–8863. $9.98 each.

The Twinkling Star. Umm Kulthumm. Long-playing record or cassette tape. Distributor: Ladyslipper. Order no.: Voix de l'Orient 42 (record), C-42 (tape). $9.95.

ISLAM

Islam and Politics in the Persian Gulf. James A. Bill. Produced by the Johnson Foundation. 1984. 30 minutes. Cassette tape. Conversations from Wingspread Series. Distributor: the Johnson Foundation. Order no.: R-1038. $4.

Islamic Women of the Middle East. Yvonne Yazbeck Haddad and Audrey Shabbas. Produced by the Johnson Foundation. 1984. 30 minutes. Cassette tape. Conversations from Wingspread Series. Distributor: the Johnson Foundation. Order no.: R-1031. $4.

IRAN

American Hostages in Iran. Reverend Jack Bremer. 1980. 30 minutes. Cassette tape. Distributor: Great Atlantic Radio Conspiracy. Order no.: 23–1180–304. $5 (individuals), $8.50 (institutions).

Folk Songs and Dances of Iran. Long-playing record. International Series. Distributor: Folkways. Order no.: 8856. $9.98.

Iran. Don Luce and Reza Baraheni. 1979. 30 minutes. Cassette tape. Distributor: Great Atlantic Radio Conspiracy. Order no.: 19–179–248. $5 (individuals), $8.50 (institutions).

Kurdish Folk Music from Western Iran. Long-playing record. Ethnic Series. Distributor: Folkways. Order no.: 4103. $10.98.

TURKEY

Folk and Traditional Music of Turkey. Long-playing record. Ethnic Series. Distributor: Folkways. Order no.: 4404. $10.98.

INFORMATION SOURCES

For additional information on audio resources related to the Middle East we suggest that you request catalogs from the distributors listed in this chapter. For tapes of radio programs, consult catalogs from the Great Atlantic Radio Conspiracy, the Johnson Foundation, and the Pacifica Radio Archive. For records, see the catalogs from Folkways, Ladyslipper, Monitor, and Paredon.

See also the publications from **Third World Resources** described in the preface to this resource directory.

Appendixes

1. UNIVERSITY CENTERS WITH
MIDDLE EAST OUTREACH PROGRAMS

The Middle East Outreach Council at the University of Utah (see address below) maintains an up-to-date list of national and regional outreach programs on the Middle East (including North Africa). The list is published in *Resource Guide for Middle Eastern Studies* (see the Catalogs, Directories, Guides section of chapter 2). The names and addresses below are excerpted from the MEOC list.

Boston University, African Studies Center, 125 Bay State Rd., Boston, MA 02215. Tel: (617) 353-7303.

Colorado State University, Office of International Education, 315 Aylesworth, Fort Collins, CO 80523. Tel: (303) 491-5917.

Duke University, Islamic and Arabian Development Studies, 2114 Campus Dr., Durham, NC 27706.

Georgetown University, Center for Contemporary Arab Studies, Community Resource Center, 501 Intercultural Center, Washington, DC 20057. Tel: (202) 625-3128.

Hartford Seminary, Duncan Black MacDonald Center for the Study of Islam and Christian-Muslim Relations, 77 Sherman St., Hartford, CT 06105. Tel: (203) 232-4451.

Harvard University, Center for Middle East Studies, Harvard Teaching Resource Center, 1737 Cambridge St., Cambridge, MA 02138. Tel: (617) 495-4078.

New York and Princeton Universities, Joint Center for Near Eastern Studies, c/o Hagop Kevorkian Center for Near Eastern Studies, 50 Washington Sq. S., New York, NY 10003. Tel: (212) 598-2697 (NYU); (609) 452-4272 (Princeton).

Ohio State University, Middle East Program, 308 Dulles Hall, 230 W. 17 Ave., Columbus, OH 43210-1367. Tel: (614) 422-9660.

Old Dominion University, South East Regional Middle East and Islamic Studies Seminar, Center for International Programs, Norfolk, VA 23508. Tel: (804) 440-4419.

State University of New York, Binghamton, Southwest Asia and North

African Program, Binghamton, NY 13901. Tel: (607) 798-2212.

Texas Tech University, Archive of Turkish Oral Narrative, University Library, Lubbock, TX 79409. Tel: (806) 742-1922.

University of Arizona, Near Eastern Center, Oriental Studies Department, Franklin Bldg., No. 80, Tucson, AZ 85721. Tel: (602) 621-5450.

University of California, Berkeley, Center for Middle Eastern Studies, 215 Moses Hall, Berkeley, CA 94720. Tel: (415) 642-8208.

University of California, Los Angeles, Von Grunebaum Center for Near Eastern Studies, 405 Hilgard Ave., Los Angeles, CA 90024. Tel: (213) 825-1571.

University of Chicago, Center for Middle Eastern Studies, 5848 S. University Ave., Chicago, IL 60637. Tel: (312) 753-4548.

University of Michigan, Outreach Program for North African and Near Eastern Studies, 144 Lane Hall, Ann Arbor, MI 48109. Tel: (313) 764-0350.

University of Minnesota, Upper Midwest Middle East Outreach Consortium, Department of History, 614 Social Sciences Bldg., 267 19 Ave. S., Minneapolis, MN 55455. Tel: (612) 373-5724.

University of Pennsylvania, Middle East Center, 838 Williams Hall/CU, Philadelphia, PA 19104. Tel: (215) 898-6335.

University of Southern California, School of International Relations, Center for Public Education in International Affairs, Los Angeles, CA 90089-0043. Tel: (213) 743-4214.

University of Texas, Middle East Resource Center, Center for Middle Eastern Studies, SSB 3.122, Austin, TX 78712. Tel: (512) 471-3881.

University of Utah, Middle East Outreach Council, Bldg. 413, Salt Lake City, UT 84112. Tel: (801) 581-6181.

University of Washington, Near East Resource Center, 318 Thompson Hall (DR-05), Seattle, WA 98105. Tel: (206) 543-7236.

2. RELIGIOUS ORGANIZATIONS WITH MIDDLE EAST INTERESTS

For information on religious organizations in North America, see the *Yearbook of American and Canadian Churches,* prepared and edited in the Office of Research, Evaluation, and Planning of the National Council of Churches (USA), 475 Riverside Dr., Rm. 876, New York, NY 10115. The 1987 edition, which contains 300 pages, was edited by Constant H. Jacquet, Jr. (Nashville, Tenn.: Abingdon Press, 1987).

Consult the *Official Catholic Directory* for names, addresses, and telephone numbers of North American Roman Catholic missionary organizations with personnel in the Middle East.

The head office of the Middle East Council of Churches is located in the Deeb Bldg. on Makhoul Street in Beirut, Lebanon. Mailing address: P.O. Box 5376. Tel: 344894. *Handbook: Member Churches of the World Council of Churches,* edited by Ans J. van der Bent, contains a list of WCC member churches in the Middle East (pp. 195–208). The revised edition of the handbook (1985) is available from the World Council of Churches, 1211 Geneva 20, Switzerland.

The churches listed below are members of the Middle East Committee, Division of Overseas Ministries, National Council of Churches (USA). The Middle East Office of the NCC is located at 475 Riverside Dr., Rm. 614, New York, NY 10115. Tel: (212) 870–2811.

American Baptist Churches, P.O. Box 851, Valley Forge, PA 19481. Tel: (215) 768–2212.

Church of the Brethren, 1451 Dundee Ave., Elgin, IL 60120. Tel: (312) 742–5100.

Coptic Orthodox Church of St. Mark, 427 West Side Ave., Jersey City, NJ 07304. Tel: (201) 333–0004.

The Episcopal Church, Episcopal Church Center, 815 Second Ave., New York, NY 10017. Tel: (212) 867–8400, ext. 373.

Friends United Meeting, 245 Second St., NE, Washington, DC 20002. Tel: (202) 547–6000.

Greek Orthodox Archdiocese, 8 E. 79 St., New York, NY 10021. Tel: (212) 570–3500.

Lutheran Church in America, 231 Madison Ave., New York, NY 10115. Tel: (212) 696–6811.

Presbyterian Church (U.S.A.), 341 Ponce de Leon Ave., NE, Atlanta, GA 20208. Tel: (404) 873–1530; 475 Riverside Dr., Rm. 1144, New York, NY 10115. Tel: (212) 870–2582. Note: the Presbyterian Church is planning to consolidate its national offices in Louisville, Kentucky, in 1988.

Reformed Church in America, 475 Riverside Dr., Rm. 1826, New York, NY 10115. Tel: (212) 870–2853.

United Church Board for World Ministries, 475 Riverside Dr., 16th floor, New York, NY 10115. Tel: (212) 870–2835.

The United Methodist Church, Board of Global Ministries, World Division, 475 Riverside Dr., Rm. 1531, New York, NY 10115. Tel: (212) 870–3701.

United Methodist Committee on Relief, 475 Riverside Dr., Rm. 1374, New York, NY 10115. Tel: (212) 870–3811.

Indexes

ORGANIZATIONS

This index contains the names of all organizations associated with the production and/or distribution of resources included in this directory. Prefixes in Arabic names, such as "Al-," are disregarded in the alphabetization. Thus, "Al-Haq" appears in the "H" section. See the Subjects Index below for references to organizations not directly connected to those resources. Addresses are provided whenever they were judged to be necessary for the acquisition of resources in this directory. Page numbers in bold face signify that the organization's address will be found in the text.

INDIVIDUALS

This index contains the names of all individuals associated with the production of resources included in this directory. See the Subjects Index below for references to individuals not directly connected to those resources.

TITLES

This index contains the names of all the print and audiovisual resources included in this directory. Alphabetization follows the logic of the computer. Search for entries in this order: Israel/Israel's/Israel-/Israel:/. Prefixes in Arabic names, such as "Al-," are disregarded in the alphabetization. Thus, "Al-Haq" appears in the "H" section. The distributor's address appears either in the text or in the Organizations Index when we have judged that the resource would not easily be available through a library or bookstore.

138   INDEXES

GEOGRAPHICAL AREAS

This index includes all references to countries and regions mentioned in this resource directory. Names are given as they appear in the resource and imply no political judgment about the legitimacy of national claims. Regional references are given only when there is a resource that treats the area as a whole. References are provided for organizations in chapter 1 only if they specify a concern for a particular country.

SUBJECTS

This topical index also contains references to organizations and individuals not directly related to the production and/or distribution of resources listed in this directory. Keyword descriptions for the issue-focus of organizations in chapter 1 do not appear in this index.

DATA
CENTER

Affiliate of the Investigative Resource Center
464 19th St., Oakland, CA 94612 USA (415) 835-4692

The Data Center is an independent, non-profit research and information center. Founded in 1977 the Center provides a range of products and services for the public-interest community on national and international issues of justice and peace.

Custom Research Services

Clipping Service: Data Center staff will monitor and clip any or all of the 400 newspapers and magazines they receive for those who need ongoing information about a given topic, such as human rights in the Philippines.

Search Service: Data Center researchers will search over 400 file drawers of periodical clippings and provide full-text photocopies of articles on corporations, countries, industries, labor issues, and a variety of other political and economic subjects.

Call or write for cost estimates on the Center's custom research services.

Publications

Latin America and Caribbean: The Center produces two regular publications on these regions: *Information Services on Latin America* (monthly) and the *Central America Monitor* (biweekly). Write for a free brochure. The Center has also compiled velo-bound collections of newsclippings on Grenada (1983, 150pp.), Jamaica (1985, 115pp.), and the Sanctuary Movement (1985, 70pp.). $10 each.

Corporate Information Services: The Center publishes two monthly 100-page collections of newspaper and magazine articles on corporate issues: *Corporate Responsibility Monitor* and *Plant Shutdowns Monitor.* Write for subscription rates. Data Center *Corporate Profiles* are custom-designed collections of articles from the media and of government and corporate documents on any of 5,000 U.S. and foreign corporations. Write for rates.

The Data Center also publishes well-organized and up-to-date collections of newsclippings on the political and religious right, terrorism, U.S. foreign policy, and environmental pollution.

The Data Center is a member-supported organization. Write for a schedule of fees and a list of benefits. Contributions are tax-deductible.

Third World Resources

464 19th Street   Oakland, CA 94612

Third World Resources gathers, catalogs, annotates, and publicizes education and action resources from and about the Third World.

Resource Directories

Twelve directories are being compiled on these subjects:

Third World general	Food, hunger, agribusiness
Africa	Human rights
Asia & Pacific	Militarism, peace, disarmament
Latin America & Caribbean	Native peoples & natural resources
Middle East	Nuclear arms & energy
Women in the Third World	TNCs & labor

Quarterly Newsletter

The *Third World Resources* newsletter contains notices and descriptive listings of organizations and newly released print, audiovisual, and other educational resources on Third World regions and issues. Inquire for subscription rates. Sample copy: US $1.

Each 16-page issue contains a unique 4-page insert with a comprehensive listing of resources on one particular region or subject. Inquire about discounts for bulk purchases.

Documentation Center

All resources are cataloged and integrated into the library collection of the Data Center where they are accessible to Center library users and Search Service clients. Bibliographical data are stored in a computerized data base to facilitate identification and retrieval of cross-referenced resources.

Third World Resources is a financially independent project of the Data Center, a non-profit, tax-exempt (501.c.3) resource center. Contributions to Third World Resources are tax-deductible.

THIRD WORLD RESOURCES

**A QUARTERLY REVIEW OF RESOURCES
FROM & ABOUT THE THIRD WORLD**

Keep the invaluable information in this resource directory complete, correct, and up-to-date by subscribing to *Third World Resources* (ISSN 8755-8831).

Third World Resources provides descriptions and capsule reviews of organizations, books, periodicals, pamphlets, audiovisual, and other education and action resources on Third World regions and issues. Entries include complete ordering information and are indexed annually. The Editors' Notes column contains updates and corrections of information published in each of the resource directories in the 12-volume set.

Each issue of the 16-page newsletter contains a unique 4-page pullout with comprehensive listings of resources on one Third World region or issue. Available at bulk discounts, these 4-page guides are excellent inexpensive handouts for talks, workshops, and study programs.

THIRD WORLD RESOURCES

**A QUARTERLY REVIEW OF RESOURCES
FROM & ABOUT THE THIRD WORLD**

Keep the invaluable information in this resource directory complete, correct, and up-to-date by subscribing to *Third World Resources* (ISSN 8755-8831).

Third World Resources provides descriptions and capsule reviews of organizations, books, periodicals, pamphlets, audiovisual, and other education and action resources on Third World regions and issues. Entries include complete ordering information and are indexed annually. The Editors' Notes column contains updates and corrections of information published in each of the resource directories in the 12-volume set.

Each issue of the 16-page newsletter contains a unique 4-page pullout with comprehensive listings of resources on one Third World region or issue. Available at bulk discounts, these 4-page guides are excellent inexpensive handouts for talks, workshops, and study programs.

ORDER FORM

Newsletter Subscription Form

☐ Please enter my subscription to Third World Resources at this rate:
   U.S. and Canada: ___ Organizational ($25/year) or ___ Individual ($25/two years)
   Foreign Airmail: ___ Organizational ($35/year) or ___ Individual ($40/two years)
   Note: Subscriptions run on a calendar-year basis only. Individual subscribers will receive
   a prorated refund if they decide to cancel at the end of the first year.
☐ Please send a sample copy of *Third World Resources* ($2).

Third World Resource Directory

☐ Please send _____ copy/copies of the *Third World Resource Directory: A Guide to
   Organizations and Publications.* Compiled and edited by Thomas P. Fenton and Mary
   J. Heffron. Maryknoll, N.Y.: Orbis Books, 1984, 304pp. $17.95. Add (per copy): $1.50
   for postage in North America; $2.50 for book rate postage overseas; $6 for airmail
   overseas.
☐ Enclosed is information on our organization for inclusion in future resource directories
   or the *Third World Resources* newsletter.
☐ Please add my/our name to your mailing list.

NAME _____

ADDRESS _____

_____

_____

Enclosed is US$ _____ for the materials I/we ordered above. Please make check/
money order payable in U.S. dollars to **Third World Resources** and send to 464 19th Street,
Oakland, CA 94612 USA.

ORDER FORM

Newsletter Subscription Form

☐ Please enter my subscription to Third World Resources at this rate:
   U.S. and Canada: ___ Organizational ($25/year) or ___ Individual ($25/two years)
   Foreign Airmail: ___ Organizational ($35/year) or ___ Individual ($40/two years)
   Note: Subscriptions run on a calendar-year basis only. Individual subscribers will receive
   a prorated refund if they decide to cancel at the end of the first year.
☐ Please send a sample copy of *Third World Resources* ($2).

Third World Resource Directory

☐ Please send _____ copy/copies of the *Third World Resource Directory: A Guide to
   Organizations and Publications.* Compiled and edited by Thomas P. Fenton and Mary
   J. Heffron. Maryknoll, N.Y.: Orbis Books, 1984, 304pp. $17.95. Add (per copy): $1.50
   for postage in North America; $2.50 for book rate postage overseas; $6 for airmail
   overseas.
☐ Enclosed is information on our organization for inclusion in future resource directories
   or the *Third World Resources* newsletter.
☐ Please add my/our name to your mailing list.

NAME _____

ADDRESS _____

_____

_____

Enclosed is US$ _____ for the materials I/we ordered above. Please make check/
money order payable in U.S. dollars to **Third World Resources** and send to 464 19th Street,
Oakland, CA 94612 USA.